How To Drown In An Empty Swimming Pool

By

Cory Flament

Dedication

This book is dedicated to my Mom who always dreamed big and encouraged me to do the same.

My wife, Brittany who always believes I can do what I say and to my daughters, Daniella, Breanna, and Corianna.

Acknowledgment

I would like to thank my 12th grade English teacher for allowing me to read this book to the class for credit and the countless people I met along the way who would listen to me read for countless hours, my editing team, my wife who encouraged me to rewrite the entire book about 20 years after the initial draft. This book would not die!

Most importantly, all praise to God!

About the Author

Cory Flament brings a wealth of life experience to his debut as an author. With a remarkable 20-year career in the Navy behind him, Cory's journey has taken him from the shores of Utica, New York, his hometown, to destinations around the globe. Now, settled in the vibrant community of Niagara Falls, New York, Cory finds inspiration in his family life, sharing his home with his beloved wife and three cherished daughters.

Beyond his dedication to his family and country, Cory harbors a passionate ambition: to see his written words come alive on the silver screen. His dream of transforming his book into a screenplay reflects not only his creative vision but also his unwavering determination to reach new heights in storytelling.

At the core of Cory's ethos lies a simple yet powerful mantra: "Motivation is free, execution is priceless." This philosophy underscores his approach to life, driving him forward in pursuit of his aspirations with relentless fervor.

With his debut work, Cory Flament invites readers into his world, crafting a narrative that resonates with authenticity and passion.

Prologue

If my life were a movie, I would have liked to be the character who gets everything he wants. You know that perfect hero, the unlikely underdog, the one that gets the girl at the end and saves the day. The guy everyone is rooting for. But as usual, I never get what I ask for. Instead, I'm pretty much the villain, the worst person I could be: I sell drugs, I inflict violence on people, and simply put, my give-a-shit meter is low. I've run out of all the shits I could give and pretty much regret every choice I ever made. I wish I could talk to my mom in times like these 'cause she would find a way to fix everything.

Look at me; I'm almost eighteen and still looking for mommy when shit hits the fan. Pretty pathetic, right? That's not how I imagined my life to turn out, though – no one does. I thought I'd get back on track by eighteen, but the reality is far from it. The truth is, I'm pretty deep into the drug trade with no exit in sight. The only exit I knew just closed up on me.

When we were kids, Mom always made waffles for breakfast on Sundays. I could still smell the sweet air around the house. When you're a kid, waffles for breakfast or really anything sugary for breakfast is just about the best damn thing. That's how simple things were back then; did Mom make your favorite food? Best day ever. Did Dad bring you home something on his way from work? Best day ever. Got sprinkles on your ice cream cone? Best day ever. Just about every day was the best day ever. I must have used up all my best days when I was young 'cause all I've been getting ever since I turned ten are shitty days – just about eight consecutive years of straight setbacks, one after the other. Constant disappoint can break a pure soul; I became a liar, cheater, drug dealer, and now even a thief.

Yeah, I even committed a robbery, you must be thinking, what kind of scum does that? This kind, the kind who got involved with drug lords and now his ass is on the line – at this point, it was either robbing or straight-up suicide 'cause I'd be damned if I sat here waiting to find out what Tony planned to do with me. I shifted into pure survival mode, and I did what I had to do to survive. On this side of the world, if you don't kill, you die. It's them or you. Roll a shitty dice enough times, and anyone can end up on this side. We're all just a few rolls away from having an entirely different life.

For some reason, I'm thinking about all the good times in my life: my mom, my dad, the idea of what I thought was a perfect family and most of all this idea of hope. Growing up with my sister Evelyn, making forts under the kitchen table, telling her stories of how things were before she was born, hoping pops would someday come back and be there for us. She never understood why I even mentioned him; after all, he was nothing but a deadbeat to her and now a fictitious name on a birth certificate. I remember having early morning and late night talks with my mom, dreaming about our family's future and her reassurance that we weren't giving up even when she had to move us to the shelter.

She never lost hope, and I guess Evelyn at the time did, or maybe she just had to learn differently than I did. She was the type where if you told her she was not to touch something because it would burn her, she would most definitely touch it and blame the person who warned her, all screaming and pointing, the complete theatrics. I was the opposite: I believed everything I heard and saw, which may be why life disappointed me. It seemed as if life was filled with lies to keep you looking for the truth, and the closer you got to the truth, the harder it was to face it because, in the end, we're all dead anyway.

Why am I thinking about this now? The sweet smell of waffles, the musical notes of my dad, the warm sun rays shining through the leaves of the trees down by the falls during my only childhood vacation – it's like all my senses are filled with nostalgia, or more like ghosts from the past. It's funny how, when you're at the end, you find yourself circling back to the beginning. Ending? Oh ya, this is the ending, I guess. I was hiding…. man, see, I can't do anything right; I almost spoiled my whole story. I suppose if you made it this far, my life is something people want to read about; I would prefer you learn from me than make the same choices I did. I am Kevin V. Turner, and this is How to Drown in an Empty Swimming Pool.

CONTENTS

Chapter 1

I Never Get What I Ask For

Over the years, I've learned nobody cares, like at a fast-food restaurant. No matter how much you stress no mustard, it seems natural for them to forget. People just don't care; it's almost like we've all become zombies living out our mundane existence, just sleepwalking through it all and don't expect any kindness or a thank you. Where I'm from, the most you get is "Be safe", as if danger is awaiting you. You're walking down the street, and out of nowhere, someone just has to ruin your day by screaming, "Fuck you," for no good reason, or you're in a store when you decide, damn, I forgot the soap, you ask the cashier, "Can I go back to get this?" most of the time they have the patience to wait. Still, it's always the rude jerk behind you who mumbles, "Asshole." I get it; maybe I need to get my shit together, but that doesn't make me an asshole. If that son of a bitch only knew…

These types of things bother me. I even struggle with life itself. Sometimes, I feel like God put us on this earth just to toy with us and see how much we can take before we ultimately break and beg for forgiveness or decide that we aren't going to play this sick game and take things into our own hands vowing to do whatever the fuck it takes to make it out of the shithole, yeah and this is where God intervenes. If we are lucky enough, we get one more chance to do the right thing or face the ultimate consequence. But I never get what I ask for. I asked for comedy, and all I got was tragedy. I asked for love, and all I got was a broken heart. I asked to live forever, but as you know, I never get what I ask for.

I mean, it hasn't quite happened yet, but yup, like you and me, everyone's going to die, some sooner than others, but it's coming for us all. I tried to be the model person, the straight-A student, the best in class, but the truth is the system expects you to fuck up anyways. You're probably thinking, *hey, that's not true,* then why the hell do we have police, jails, and prison? Are they just landmarks used in case of emergencies? Nope, wrong again; their sole purpose is to house criminals who were once innocent babies with no intention to do wrong; who am I kidding? Some of the people, it's almost like they were born evil. As if evil was ingrained in their DNA, spawns of Satan in some cases, and some people like me. If you were to look at us in a lineup,

I'm ashamed, but you wouldn't be able to tell who was who. I can promise you this: I have a good heart, I guess, ultimately, it's the age-old question of nurture versus nature, what has the most influence, who I am is the result.

Not to mention the problem of the world that most people don't care about, like, poverty, drugs, and the threat of world destruction; to tell you the truth, I don't give a damn either, well not anymore, I bet you think that's a little too harsh. Well, live with it. Don't get me wrong, I used to be one of those kids who tried hard to change the world, but it's ironic because the world changed me instead.

The evolution began on June 14, 1985, at Kings County Hospital in Brooklyn, New York; about midnight, I came to life. I was born to a happily married couple, Cleveland and Sandra Turner. My life seemed to start perfectly. My parents were married in the pursuit of happiness, and they now had a son whom they named Kevin Volton Turner. I know the middle name sounds funny, but don't ask. My parents just wanted to give me a middle name, or maybe it was their way of ensuring my story would be unique or pointless. The early years were incredible; my mother was more than I could ask for. She took me places, talked to me constantly, and baked the best chocolate chip cookies. I'm not talking just cookies; I'm talking walnuts and M&M's, the stay-chewy type. I can still hear her say softly, "Kevin, you're the best gift I could ask for, and remember, you are bound for greatness," as I took a bite of the warm cookie, with the aroma of wholesome goodness filling the desire between each bite. Just thinking back to the good old days gives me a sense of euphoria.

My pops, well, I guess most would look at him as a dreamer with big goals and full of hope. It's funny, looking back, the only thing I remember about my dad was that he loved two things: his keyboard and the music it played. Every day, he would play a new beat and tell me to bust a rap. I never could get going, he would take the mic, and suddenly, it was as if he was in a filled arena as he performed. My dad spent a lot of time with me in the early days. He would take me down to Prospect Park, and as we lay in the grass, he would look at me and say, "Look at all this beauty, Kev. If you ever need a reminder of God's power, this is it, never let dem tell ya no different".

I must be honest, I never really understood what he meant back then. I grew up in a brownstone in Brooklyn, yeah, we have parks and trees, but most people forget to look around, and I think that's why this place I called home is referred to as the concrete jungle. The area I grew up was called little Italy, my mom was mixed, Italian and Puerto Rican, and my pops was Island mulatto. His family migrated from Trinidad and Tobago when my father was a junior in high school. People would always ask me "what I am" and I would reply human. I was so naïve, what they really wanted to know was, if I was black or not. I never really had a cultural identity growing up, never black enough and damn sure not white or Italian enough, but my neighborhood, with its share of poverty and crime, in the middle of "God's beauty", as pops would say, still felt like home, maybe because it was the only home I knew.

My dad always made it a point to repeat the exact quote every chance he got, "One day, you're going to be the best. One day, you will even be better than me, but today is not that day, son." I would eventually say it with him in harmony as he put what seemed to be a giant hand on my head. With a little pat, he would head out the door and say,

"Lil man, daddy's gonna make a hit today" (my pops was in the music business), and my mom would yell, "Remember the rent is due next week, love ya!" He would reply with a dramatic change in tone as if his soul was crushed by God, "I know… I'm on the verge of greatness; you'll see, babe. Love you too," Dad sighed.

I didn't see much of my dad after about six years old; chasing his dream kept him away from home. I believed in everything back then, like the perfect life, family, and future; I guess I lived what Dr. King must have envisioned when he pinned his iconic "I Have a Dream" speech. My parents seemed to grow further apart as I got older, but deep down, I still believed our family would return to the picnics in the park, which gave me a feeling of nostalgia I craved.

I can just about smell the grass and the texture of the football for the first time. I must have been 4 or 5, and I can still hear my dad yelling with excitement, "Kevin, you caught your first pass!" It's like every milestone was a teachable moment on hope and progress. I guess hope is just a part of growing up, and sometimes, the picnics are short-lived and suddenly rained out. It wasn't until my mother gave birth to my sister, Evelyn, that I realized life wasn't meant to be perfect; the day my sister was born was the same day our father walked out of our lives forever. At the time, it seemed like he was always one day from returning, but the days turned into years, and the pain eventually turned to hatred at the thought of him. I just couldn't understand why he would leave my mom to struggle with two kids while he went off to follow his dreams. I wanted my dad back. The day he left, I got this sunken feeling in my chest and what I would describe as a gulp in my throat, almost like I was trying to swallow a golf ball; this is a feeling I still have to this day. I would ask my mom if she wondered where Dad was or if he ever made a hit record.

She would just say, "Your dad loves you and there is a reason for everything. I'm sure he is still chasing his dreams." I used to be mad at her, too, then. How could she be so calm about the situation? I mean, your husband just left you to raise two two kids alone! How could she remain so calm in this moment? I felt like no one understood my pain and for the first time in my life, I felt alone. I prayed every night for my dad to come back or at least for God to give me a sign that he still loved me. I thought I was the only one with pain, that was until Evelyn grew up. Her rage made mine look like a spark against an atomic bomb. But my mom was always so calm about the situation, it was almost like she completely understood why my dad left or why Evelyn lost her shit every time something didn't go her way. She would always change the subject when I brought up the idea of looking for my dad or contacting his side of the family, who had relocated to Florida. You can only judge people when the stress is great; I believed that whatever caused him to leave could be fixed with something as simple as sorry.

I cried often and thought he was a weak man, leaving my mom to struggle with two kids with little money and no explanation for his actions. I was the man of the house by default, and suddenly, a weight was placed on my shoulders. Despite it all, I just had a feeling we would be ok. My mom was a fighter, and when the times got hard, she got stronger, so we just kept pushing. She worked often and didn't get to spend much time with Evelyn like she did with me. I guess I was selfish for thinking that at least she still had a mom to look up to. Who was gonna teach me how to be a man? I mean, I still sat down to pee and pat dry. See what I mean? Moms know nothing about standing up and aiming or shaking it out. My idea of who I wanted to be turned out to be a big disappointment, probably like when you first found out the lunar landing was a hoax or that Osama Bin Laden died of natural causes; just kidding, but hopefully, you get my point. Basically, everything I knew about life was debunked like an episode of MythBusters. Growing up without your pops is tough, but enough about that for now.

In grade school, I had to fight every day. Man, I was pretty good with it, too. I never lost a fight. The kids on the block used to call me little Ali! Like Muhammad Ali. Ok! That's not true, but it sounds good; you can't blame a guy for trying to make himself look good. I mean, it is my story. The reason I had to fight was my sister, Evelyn. She always seemed to find something to run her mouth about; she pretty much had diarrhea of the mouth and didn't think twice about hurting people's feelings, and like always, I was her banker cashing the checks her mouth couldn't. I kinda understood her mean-girl attitude. She tried to look big because she knew she wasn't. Hurt people, hurt people, and that's just what she was doing. By inflicting the shame, insecurity, and hurt she felt on others, she thought maybe she could feel less of it and maybe it worked 'cause she kept doing it no matter how many times things went south.

We were pretty close, and I would tell her stories about things before she was born as we ate a bowl of ramen in our fort under the kitchen table. I guess I just wanted her to know everything she knew about our current life was temporary and it would get better. To her, though, they sounded like fairytales and wishful thinking of a little boy who still hasn't accepted reality. Maybe the thought of a better life caused her to act out. After all, mom often worked doubles just to put food on the table, fighting gets old, and being the older brother of a blabber mouth didn't help the situation.

Still, I had perseverance, and the thought of a future much like what life used to be motivated me. When things got shitty at home, I found another home at school. I'd sign up for random club activities and whatever came my way just to keep myself on track – see, I told you I tried. I didn't think about it at the time when my father left for good, but looking back, I guess you could see the writing on the walls.

I would say about a year before Eve was born I was introduced to the sound of my parents fighting and arguing, which was something entirely new to me. I guess it started around the time when Dad returned from one of his music escapades. He was on tour with an up-and-coming rapper (for legal reasons, I can't mention his name, but he turned out to be a pretty big deal.) I never really understood what they were fighting about, but I would often hear my dad say, "I'm here for Kev, I don't give a shit what you got going on, Sandy." I soon learned that Sandy was the nickname my dad called my mom when he was hurt. I also witnessed a dark side of my mom as she would throw things and scream, "I'm sorry, I just can't anymore!" After the storm came the calm and they would lock the door to their room and when they came back out, they always took me to my favorite ice cream shop at Coney Island. This made me happy and it seemed like my parents were once again the happiest people in the world. Looking back, I think they put their issues aside and seeing me happy made them happy.

That's when I learned that love alone isn't enough. It never was. That was the first lesson life taught me.

Chapter 2

The ~~Hero~~ Asshole Gets the Girl

I was a typical American kid in every sense of the word. I wanted the nicest stuff, the prettiest girl in the class, and believed that America was the greatest country in the world. We always started class with the pledge of allegiance: "I pledge allegiance to the Flag of the United States of America, and to the Republic for which it stands, one Nation under God, indivisible, with liberty and justice for all." Saying these words gave me a sense of pride. I was proud of not only who I was even with our current situation but also what my country stood for: freedom and justice. This reminded me that I still had a future as these words echoed throughout the classroom walls, and it was just something you felt much like most things before loyalty became an infringement on so-called freedom….

I almost got ahead of myself there. Well, coming back to the story.

I always tried to be the teacher's favorite. I guess it made me feel the way my mom made me feel when I was younger. I was a sucker for validation, can't blame a kid for just wanting to be seen, though. But there was always this one girl who wanted it just a bit more than I did. She is Karen Vinter, "the prettiest girl in the class." Man, did I love her, but at the same time, I hated her guts because she always seemed to beat me to teachers' hearts; I know it sounds stupid. But, my goal was to be a model person, a straight student, and the best in the class; I felt like my future depended on it. So, of course, I hated whoever stood between me and my goal. I soon realized, though, that nothing was fair, like when Karen cheated to steal my spot at the top of the class. Karen and I were head-to-head in the last round of a math competition. The rules were simple: hear the question and write the answer on the board; the question was easy. I wrote the answer first and was the winner, but we live in a cold world. In true Karen fashion, it just happened that Karen didn't hear the question; that's what she told the teacher, at least.

So the teacher gave us another problem, it wasn't hard either. But I was still mad at what just happened that I didn't even attempt to answer it, and just like that, I was screwed again out of my chance of being the smartest kid in the class. I guess that's where my tendency to fuck things up for myself started. I still could've made it, but I let my pettiness get the best of me. There were multiple situations with the same outcome. So, I guess my motivation slowly faded. I also realized that I had feelings for Karen. That also contributed to my dying passion for school; to be honest, eventually, it became the only thing that motivated me to even go to school. I spent days contemplating my thoughts, then I just said the hell with it and told her how I felt, and you know what? She kissed me! She did!

But that was just before I woke up; I was so confused. It seemed so real. You see how bad it was; I was thinking of this girl even in my sleep. I used to dream about getting appreciated by Mrs. Patt, my math teacher; when did it get to this? In my dream, she looked so perfect, so beautiful, and most importantly, deeply in love with me! It seemed that just about anything could happen in a dream. These pipe dreams inspired me to make them my reality. It looked so easy and so close! I was just one decision away from turning what I saw into an actual reality. Getting kissed by Karen in real life. Just a matter of manning up and actually confessing. Just one move away. Right? But that's not how it is in real life. Confessing is not just confessing in real life.

It comes with a lot of insecurities, what-ifs, horrible scenarios of public humiliation, the need for at least one backup plan, and so much extra baggage! In dreams, all this doesn't exist, it is all about that one moment. But I wasn't giving up anymore; I already gave my initial dream of becoming the star student, I wasn't going to give up on this one, too. I made up my mind; no more giving up!

So when the following year started, I went back to that place that I now didn't care much about, ya know, school. It's funny how my views could change in a matter of months. Well, back to what happened, I was at school walking down the hallway, determined to tell Karen how I felt, palms sweaty, heart pounding, heavy breathing – you know the drill. When I finally saw her, I attempted to talk, but all I could do was stutter and by the time I said, "Hi," it was already time to get to class. But I was in luck because my best friend, Mikey, and I got the same class. I knew if there was anyone I could talk to about Karen, it would have to be him. That was my intention, and here's how I imagined the conversation would go,

"Hey, what's up, Mikey? How was your summer?" I say, trying to act cool.

"Cool," replies Mikey.

"So what did you do?"

"Nothing much, what about you?"

"Same, bro."

"So, I gotta tell you something, man," I say, hesitating a little but still acting cool 'cause I'm a cool guy, right.

"Ya?" Mikey asks curiously.

"I kinda have this crush on Karen," I say as I scratch my head.

"Oh shit, man! Don't you like hate her or something?"

"Nah, never really did. I just didn't know how to go about my feelings."

"Wow, my man's all grown up, alright. I got you."

Then we both high-five like bros.

The End.

Now, here's how it actually went.

"Hey, what's up, Mikey? How was your summer?" I said, following the script in my head.

"Cool," Mikey replied, and I was already feeling confident. He coulda said so many things in reply to that, but he said cool, as I predicted. So, I felt like the rest of the scenario in my head was going to flow just as smoothly.

"So, what did you do?"

"Well, first my dad had to go overseas for a business meeting, so my mom took me and my sister to Wonderland down in Florida," Mikey replied and this is where reality smacked me in my face like a pimp I owed money to. Because first, my mom never takes us anywhere, and second, he wasn't following the damn script!

"Man, I wish my mom could've taken me and my sister there," I said, keeping my calm while thinking to myself that there was no way in hell my mom could afford a trip like that. Even though I was envious, I made it seem like we just didn't get the chance to go.

Mikey carelessly carried on, "It sucked, I wish my dad was there," again another response that made me feel weak. At least he has his dad, I thought to myself, and he continued… "But after we got back, my sister got invited to Karen's party. It was great. I know how you feel about her and all, but she's not that bad. Actually, I think I kind of like her."

Wait, what? I felt that damn golf ball in my throat again. Not only was he WILDLY off the script, but he was also coming for Karen!

"WOW! Wait a second, how could you like her?" I tried my best to sound disgusted, but I thought this had to be the worst thing that could happen. My best friend was in love with my girl; how could this be? Talk about being a loser! He didn't let my disgust mold his feelings, though. He continued telling me just how amazing he found her. After I heard him express his feelings for Karen, I was so angry I couldn't stand the words that just came out of his mouth. My best friend was now nothing but a lowdown, girl-stealing sucker. Yeah, he had a point, I must have shown the world that I hated her, but the war deep inside my heart was about to start. Should I support him, or should I go for it myself?

I swallowed my emotion, feeling the "golf ball" pain intensify, and said, "Go for it, man. Wish you luck." I died inside, but my nature is to be the bigger person. No need to tell the truth and as my mom would say, "be set free," right?

Thinking back at that phrase, she would have Eve and I put our hand on the Bible and say, "The truth will set me free." I believed that if I lied with my hand on the Bible, I would be instantly struck by lightning, well that was until I watched Evelyn throw a shoe at my mom's TV and decide to lie about it, I watched her throw the shoe and she smiled in my face and said, "I can prove it." I ran and got the Bible. She smiled and said with her hand firmly placed on the great book, "Dear God, I did not throw the shoe, but you already know that because, well, you are the all-mighty God, right?" She said with a smirk and just like that, my last checkpoint for being an honest person admonished as Evelyn laughed and said, "See! Kev, either God is not real, or he loves me so much that nothing happens when I do bad things."

I mean, I was a bit relieved when nothing happened, I thought she was about to be literal toast, but hey, I'm thankful God spared her, if he is real, that is, not gonna lie,

I kinda leaned more towards the latter… damn I got off track again.

Back to Mikey.

It's not like he knew about my feelings or anything. So it wasn't his fault, but I was petty.

"See you around," I couldn't stand facing him anymore. I was afraid that if we talked any longer, I'd say something I'd end up regretting later.

"See you, Turner," Mikey said before walking away with a swift peace sign. Ok, that's it. That right there was another thing I hated – people calling me by my last name as if my first name wasn't worthy enough. It was game on! Now that I look back on it, I guess I should have told Mikey about my feelings for Karen. But the choice was clear back then: either kick Mikey to the curb or let Karen know how I felt about her, to let her decide. So I ended up writing her a note:

Dear Karen,

Hi, it's me, Kevin.

How was your summer? Mine was great. Well, I'm writing to you because I wanted to apologize for how I acted toward you. And I like you. Do you like me? (Circle your answer)

YES

NO

Sincerely yours,

Kevin V. Turner

I gave that letter to her, and she smiled as she returned it to me. I opened it eagerly and saw a big circle on "yes." This time, she actually kissed me. I was on cloud nine, man. I had never experienced something like that. Love has got to be the strongest drug known to man 'cause I got hooked right off the bat! Suddenly, I was the main character. I mean, it's always the hero who gets the girl, right? I was the hero; everything was better for a while. Grades falling? Who cares? I bagged the prettiest girl in the class every guy wanted; I already won. Even troubles at home seemed small. No matter how shitty my day was going, I could just call Karen any time, and she'd lift up my spirits like magic. That's until I would hear a giggle on the line and had to tell Eve to hang up the other phone. No matter how bad things were, at the end of the day, I always had a place I could go to where I was the hero. It felt great. I was so lost in the love spell I didn't bother talking to Mikey. I gave all my time to Karen.

So, at the same time, I also experienced the sadness of losing a friend. After Mikey found out, he didn't say much to me; I understood. I mean, it was a pretty shitty move to go ahead and confess to the girl your best friend just told you he had feelings for. And to top it off, you also wished him luck instead of telling him about what was going on in your head. It was a pretty crappy thing to do. I felt terrible, but I had to follow my heart. My mind was made up: I won't let anyone stop me from getting the things I want. I guess you could say I started to take my destiny into my own hands. I guess that's where my true evolution began; I was sick of praying and waiting for God to save me. It was only the beginning of the many things I'd do with the same mindset.

Here's a little side note before I forget, being motivational and ambitious is good; go for the things you want, but don't make asshole moves like this one I just made and the many that I'm about to make as you read.

In true-asshole fashion, I didn't talk to Mikey for months. I was happily love-struck, living with my perfect girlfriend in my fantasy world. It wasn't until I experienced yet another letdown and broke up with Karen for kissing another boy behind my back about a year later that I realized I had made the wrong choice. So now I was on the quest to set the record straight and get my friend, Mikey, back. I felt terrible about the choice I made, so I talked to him about it. Surprisingly, he was relaxed about the whole thing.

"I just find it funny, man, that you let a girl come between us." He chuckled like it was nothing, and I smiled sheepishly at him. Man, I felt so stupid and wanted to make amends so I invited him on our family trip – the only trip my family ever took, actually. It was a trip to Niagara Falls, NY. My mom was raised in Niagara Falls and grew up in an apartment on the corner of Pine and 26th. I couldn't believe my mom's hood was just blocks away from one of the world's most beautiful places. I had to shovel snow for the neighbors for weeks just so I could bring him, knowing that my mom had saved since this time last year so we could afford this trip. (I loved my mom; she always worked hard to put food on the table) I couldn't dare ask her to pay for Mikey. It was hard enough already. So, I made up my mind to earn all one hundred and forty dollars myself so he could come along. Man, how I wanted to keep that money or at least give it to my mom to help out! But, like I said, I was on a quest; I wanted Mikey to know I was a true friend and truly wanted to make up for being such an asshole.

The trip was a hit, and I caught up on lost time; how could I almost forget my best friend? Boy, did he change? He was much taller than me and even started to grow a mustache; I barely had peach fuzz. He forgave me, but the truth is I didn't forgive myself just yet, like they say, "time heals all wounds," that proved true. In a matter of weeks, we were best friends again, and the following summer, Mikey's family went to Europe. I can't say this was the best summer; I kind of just stayed inside the house and kept to myself; well, not really. I still had Evelyn, but she grew up fast. That was the summer when Evelyn and I discovered 20 Oz Sprite and strawberry shortcake ice cream.

We walked to the corner store every afternoon after we begged our mom for a few food stamps. I always got Evelyn to check out because I was a little embarrassed to use poor people's money. Looking back, most people I lived around had the same money, but none of us admitted it. I guess you could say we were proud people who fell on rough times. I guess it's because I remember when my mom often gauged our poverty level by saying, "At least we're not on food stamps," Now, when we were, she shifted to saying, "At least we still have a roof over our head." I was already worried that she had jinxed it and that she'd soon have to come up with a new measurement for our level of poverty. My parents bought our Brownstone home from one of our elderly family members who believed in what my parents were starting, and it was my mom's goal to keep that house in the family. I even used this status to defend my thrift store clothes when other kids would make fun of me. The truth is we never really owned anything as my mom struggled to keep up with the taxes, and I often found her at the kitchen table reading the tax statement that warned of a looming tax foreclosure, among other bills.

I would ask my mom, "Is there anything I can do to help?"

She would smile and say, "We're going to be ok."

I seriously doubted that.

Chapter 3
Just When You Think You Know Everything

It was the last week of August when Mikey got back; he had so many stories of his incredible fucking family vacation with emphasis on the "fucking" – he changed on me again. He smoked and claimed to have lost his virginity like any fourteen-year-old. I was curious; I asked him questions like how was it? Was it easy? Did you wrap it up? The way he described it made it seem as if sex was better than life itself. Come to think of it, Mickey pretty much described it like a porno, I was convinced at the time, but honestly, looking back on it, he probably made it up. My guy probably just watched a lot of porn and let his imagination run wild. Whatever the truth was, I wasn't looking to find out. I lost a lot up to this point in my life, but I still had my morals; I vowed never to use drugs and wait until I was married to find out about what it feels like to, you know, have sex. I knew there had to be more to it than just a good feeling, like Mikey made it seem like. I mean, being with someone in such a way requires a certain level of vulnerability and connection, right? To be so close and all up in someone's business like that must require some sort of spiritual connection. I was such an idealist; I romanticized everything. For me, sex meant more than just rubbing flesh together.

Yeah… I almost got off track again.

Let's see where I was. Yeah, so Mikey and I were tight again, but being a big bro was still a full-time gig, you know? Couldn't stick to Mikey 24/7 with middle school and all that jazz. And yeah, I actually dug it there. Evelyn, as per usual, was a magnet for trouble, and I did what I could to keep things smooth. But honestly, I love my sis to bits, no matter what.

After dealing with her drama for what felt like forever, it was about time to get real with her. Even if it just meant telling her to zip it for once. And that's exactly what I did. Man, did she blow up at me or what? Called me every name under the sun. I was like, "Seriously? After all the times I've had your back?" Maybe she's just hardwired to be a pain. I was ticked off, sure, and I let her know it, but deep down, I'm still her bro. She might not have seen it then, but she'd need me again, and I'd be there. Didn't say that part out loud, though.

Middle school? Flew by in a blink. Mikey and I hung out at the mall, checking out the scene. We were past being just friends—we were bros. Mikey was the smooth talker, the ladies' man, and then there was me, the guy who stayed out of trouble and was too chicken to chat up the girls. Sometimes, I'd let Evelyn tag along. Mikey was cool with it; she was practically his sis too. We were so tight we even called each other's moms 'Mom.' That summer before high school, I was stepping up, not a kid anymore but not quite an adult either.

June 22, 1999, the kickoff to a summer I'd end up hating. Started off like any other—me at the mall, babysitting Evelyn, chilling with Mikey. Even snagged a job to help Mom out since we were this close to losing the house, and her paycheck wasn't cutting it. Not having the latest gear didn't bug me much, but for Evelyn, it was a big deal. So she started lifting stuff from stores. Turned out she was a natural at it. One day, she came home loaded with new clothes and kicks. Mom was all, "Where'd you get this?"

Evelyn played it cool. "Won a shopping spree on the radio."

Mom bought it, happy as can be, 'cause she knew how much it meant to Evelyn. But I knew the score. Evelyn wasn't winning contests; she was swiping stuff. I wasn't mad, just bummed out about it.

I decided to confront her, being the big brother and the man of the house, you know. So I walked into her room and said, "I know how you got these, Evelyn."

Not a single shade of shame on her face, "Ya, and?"

"And what?! You're going to get Mom upset?"

"Oh, come on! She'd only be upset if she knew. Now, you wouldn't be so mean to tell her and break her heart, would you?"

What a devil, this girl.

"You're hopeless." I sighed and walked out. What a man-of-the-house talk there. Great work. I patted myself sarcastically on the back.

That's just who Evelyn was, she just did what made her happy, but just like all good things come to an end, so did Evelyn's random shopping sprees when she got caught one day. Yeah, good for her, right, but it wasn't her who I was worried about. Mom was the one who struggled to make the best of what we had, buying clothes for us if only her boss would let her work extra hours on the weekend, supporting us paycheck to paycheck all these years, so I couldn't possibly imagine letting her feel like even after all that, she failed. When the police called, call it luck or divine intervention because it was out of pure coincidence that it was I who answered the phone.

I've been anticipating this call, so I knew what to do, I immediately started pleading to let her go. They were kind enough to listen but on one condition, "Just keep her out of the mall, son." My mom didn't hear anything about my sister's problem. I took it upon myself to save her the heartbreak, this still didn't solve the issue at hand and make money magically appear in my mom's paycheck. It was only a matter of time and the time was here, the city foreclosed on our house, we were broke and in the worst financial state of my life. We hit a new low, and I was not ready for it. Just when I was thinking, I could actually help Mom with my job and there was a way out of this rut, life pushed me back even harder. It felt personal, like the universe really gave me the middle finger.

We found ourselves, for the first time, homeless, living in The House of Eve, a run-down family shelter. I was so embarrassed to be living in a shelter I just told Mickey that we were going out of town and wouldn't be returning until the end of summer. I can't have him seeing my family like this, not in a million years. It was not because I thought Mikey would judge or find me less of a friend, I knew him to be better. But it was my own pride that didn't allow me to tell him anything about this. I guess we want our friends to see us as equals – not less, not more. Just someone you see as a reflection. Companionship is built with people we respect to be our equals, after all. You know, the entire birds-of-the-feather-flock-together or some shit. So ya, I just told him we wouldn't see each other until we "get back into town or find a new place to live," that much was true.

The shelter wasn't that bad, actually, and surprisingly, Evelyn even made a few friends with the other homeless kids there. We lived day to day at the shelter, they allowed my mom to work so she could save up for our new place.

She even enrolled in a college degree program in business management. Her goal was to open a restaurant someday. I saw Mom and Evelyn going about their lives as usual, and here I was, all gloomy and loopy. I missed my bro, but I was a proud man, too proud to admit it aloud, so I coped with my emotions like a man – by shoving them deep inside and not admitting them to a soul. I even quit my job when we first got to the shelter just to keep out of sight.

I thought, with the last warning, Evelyn must have learned her lesson, but these new friends at the shelter were bad news. It turned out that they too had a bad case of the sticky fingers. People like these make poor folks look bad. Yes, all of us want the finer things in life, but not all of us would go so low to get them. Well, this time, when she got caught, the mall pressed charges and escorted her back to the shelter to notify my mom. I couldn't save her this time. It's funny 'cause when the police told my mom, she was cool about the whole thing.

I mean, my mom was never one of those types that beat her kids anyway and I know my sister wishes it ended like that 'cause, man, after the cop left, Mom opened up a can of whoop-ass on Evelyn. It was almost as if she beat her for our suffering. Evelyn was due back in court about a week later, so Mom took her and she was put on probation. You would think after the embarrassment she put my mom through, she would think twice before she made the same mistake. But nope, sure enough, she got busted again about a week later after she promised my mom she would change this time.

This time, she didn't come home, though. They held her at the Children's Home of the Lower Hudson and gave Mom a chance to intervene, but she just gave my sister the cold shoulder. How could she let them take my sister just like that? That's when I realized Mom, too, could be a cruel person. I hated her for letting them take my little sis, whom I protected for all these years. How could I trust my mom after what she did to Evelyn?

For once, I couldn't understand why my mom made the choice that she did. I still loved her even though I didn't talk to her for about a week or so, and when I did, I realized that most of life is just an illusion created in the human mind because how much do we really know about each other?

Yeah, sure, we know names, birthdays, sometimes criminal records, and occasionally their favorite things and some stuff they share themself. But at the core, we may never know a person truly. We're strangers living among strangers. I felt so out of place like all connections I could ever possibly make will always be fickle – one move away from fading into nothing. Something so fragile, is it even worth keeping? Is it even worth my energy and time? I mean, why bother to build something so flimsy?

I guess my views of people really changed at this point. First, my dad walked out on us when I was young, just as Evelyn was born. I drove myself crazy, questioning the same question again and again: Why? I was old enough to remember him clearly before he left. I had such soft memories of us together that my mind would just not accept the fact that he did something like that just on a whim or for something selfish, like making it big in the industry. He was a family guy. He loved us! So what exactly went wrong here, and why won't Mom tell me anything? Was it my mom's fault, or was it Evelyn's? Or did I do something? That was a weight that I carried for a long time. Blaming and questioning myself. I sometimes looked at kids my age who came from healthy, functioning families and wondered what it felt like to live like that. To not have such things hold you back. The things I could accomplish if I wasn't weighed down by all that extra baggage. I was jealous of these other kids, I thought they had it too easy and should not whine about a single thing. I was actually mad when I saw someone from a normal family act up or be lazy; like, what the fuck is your problem, dude?

Well, life doesn't get any sweeter by being bitter at it, so I just did what I had to do. I lived day to day. Life at the shelter was mundane and monotonous. That's my idea of hell, by the way. Not torture or fiery pits, but this! The dull and grey monotony of being stuck in a loop. Feeling like there's no way out of the pit you're in no matter how much and how hard you climb. Cursed like Sisyphus to drag the same fucking boulder every day, only for it to end up at the bottom again. That is true hell. At this point, it was all kinda melting together. Was I the boulder or Sisyphus in this scenario? We've both broken down and become one. I became the weight I dragged, my identity dissolving down to nothing but the heaviness I felt inside – it was all I knew, so it was all I became. At this point in my life, I thought I knew everything about everything, this life was filled with bullshit and broken promises, I worked up the courage to con.

Chapter 4

Why God, Why?

Three months — that's how long it's been since the shelter became less of a pit stop and more like quicksand. I'd walked in with a head full of 'temporary' and watched as the days bled into each other, each one a carbon copy of the last. The thought haunted me, gnawing at the edges of my hope —what if this is as good as it gets?

The shelter was a melting pot of stories, each face a chapter of hardship — kids, the elderly, souls on the brink. They all wore the same cloak of invisibility here. Nothing much ever happened, and the stillness was suffocating.

Mom, bless her; she was still chasing her degree, clinging to the belief that it was our golden ticket out of this place. But her dreams felt like a mirage to me. I know three months is a drop in the bucket, but when you're young, it's an ocean of time. Each moment I wasn't out there, seizing life, felt like a stolen chance, a breath I wasn't taking. I was fading, each tick of the clock a reminder of what I didn't have.

Mikey's life was a stark contrast — his room, his getaways, even his damn wardrobe. I wanted it all, and it burned me up inside. Anger became my constant companion, directed at everyone — my folks, myself, even the universe. It seemed like a cruel joke, this imbalance of life. Why did some have it all while others were left craving the basics?

Dreams are supposed to be wild, right? Like gorging on ice cream without the bellyache, globe-trotting without a care, or being swarmed by beauty. They're not supposed to be about yearning for a room of your own. That's just... pathetic.

And the lies. They were piling up, one on top of the other, a house of cards waiting to collapse. I'd been avoiding Mikey, making sure he didn't get a glimpse of my reality. But how long before he noticed the cracks? Our mall days were history, thanks to Evelyn's infamous stunt. Now, every question from Mikey was a minefield, and I was the expert defuser, dodging and weaving with more lies.

Lying — it's like a snowball rolling downhill, growing bigger with every turn. You tell one, then another to cover the first, and before you know it, you're living in a fortress made of fiction. It's only a matter of time before it all comes tumbling down. And there I was, barely hanging on, scrambling for a story that could patch the holes in my crumbling castle.

"Hey, Turner!" Mikey's voice cut through the hallway din. I tried to ignore it, but his call grew louder, forcing me to face him. He weaved through the crowd, a determined look on his face.

"'Sup?" I managed, feigning nonchalance as he approached.

"Don't 'Sup' me! You've been MIA since the semester kicked off. What gives, man?"

"Ignoring you? C'mon, we're practically brothers. Why would I do that?"

"Yeah, that's what I'm trying to figure out. You said you'd be busy moving house over the holidays, so I waited, thinking you had your hands full. But this? It's getting ridiculous. Got a new bestie in your fancy neighborhood? Am I old news, Turner?" His drama was all for show, but the hurt was real. I chuckled, shaking my head. "You sound like a jealous partner. It's not like that. Listen, and keep this under wraps," I whispered, leaning in, "we're having trouble locking down a new place. Mom's picky, and with Evelyn growing up, she's eyeing a swanky area. So we're crashing at our aunt's. Kinda embarrassing, you know?" Embarrassing was an understatement. How could I admit we were holed up in a shelter with no way out? I was stalling for a miracle, anything to dodge the truth.

"I get it, man. That's rough."

"Appreciate it. But let's keep it between us, alright?"

"Cross my heart," he replied, tapping his chest with a smile.

"Catch you later, Turner."

"Later," I said, watching him blend back into the crowd. That was the last I saw of Mikey at school. A week later, he vanished from class. Concerned, I dropped by his place. His mom greeted me with silence and a nod toward his room.

"Thanks for coming," she murmured. Mikey was a ghost of himself, pale and frail. He tried to muster his usual bravado as I approached.

"Turner, my man. What's good?"

"You look like hell, dude!"

"Yeah, skipped my workout this morning," he joked, but a coughing fit seized him. I handed him water, my hand trembling as I felt his fragile frame.

"What's going on with you?"

"Just some nonsense with my heart. Docs say I'll pull through."

"That's good to hear. When you coming back to school?"

"Give it a month, maybe," he said with a shrug. I couldn't tell if he believed his own words or if it was just another brave front.

Time marches on, indifferent and relentless. A month had slipped by, and with each day, I harbored the hope of Mikey's return to school. But he remained absent, an empty seat echoing silence. Monday morning dawned, draped in its typical shroud of gloom, the collective mood of the class mirroring my own disquiet. I scanned the room for Mikey's familiar grin, the one that could cut through the dreariness of school life. Instead, a different scene unfolded.

Mrs. Collin entered, her usual stern demeanor replaced by a pallor of distress. The room fell eerily silent as she spoke, her voice a fragile whisper carrying the weight of unthinkable news.

"Class, I must share something deeply sorrowful. Michael Matthew, our dear student and your friend, passed away due to a heart complication this weekend. Let's honor his memory with a moment of silence."

The words struck like a physical blow, blurring my vision —not with confusion, but with the sudden sting of tears. They betrayed me, streaming down my face despite my frantic attempts to conceal them. In that instant, I was acutely aware of the societal chains that bind us — dictates of masculinity that label tears as weakness, that equate emotion with frailty.

As a child, my tears were met with scorn, my mother's words cutting deep, "Stop being a fag." Eve adopted the same cruel mantra, using it as a weapon whenever she pleased. To express joy too freely, to show sorrow—these were the unspoken sins of my upbringing. So, even amidst the crushing tide of grief, I fought to 'man up,' to adhere to the twisted code that demanded stoicism.

...died from a heart complication this weekend...

Mikey's assurances echoed hollowly in my mind. We all cloak our pain with lies, don't we? His untimely departure added yet another question to the growing list that haunted me. What was the true nature of his ailment? How long had he carried this secret? Why hadn't he confided in me?

Amidst the torrent of emotions, a dark thought crept in—a sense of culpability. It was I who had silently wished for Mikey to remain oblivious to my reality, to the truth of the shelter that was my refuge. And now, in the cruelest twist of fate, my selfish prayer had been granted. The irony was bitter, the realization that my desperate desire to maintain a facade had, in some twisted way, contributed to this outcome.

It all seemed so trivial now, so painfully insignificant. The lies I had clung to, the image I had so fiercely protected — all rendered meaningless by the stark finality of loss. He was my brother in all the ways that mattered; he would have understood, wouldn't he? But such thoughts were futile whispers against the void left by his absence.

He was gone.

Gone...

In the span of a heartbeat.

The day of Mikey's funeral arrived with a sky painted in shades of mourning, a canvas of gray that stretched endlessly above. The air was thick with the scent of freshly turned earth and the subtle fragrance of lilies, which adorned the somber space with their pallid beauty. The funeral home, a quiet sanctuary of final farewells, was awash in the soft glow of flickering candles, casting dancing shadows upon the walls.

As I entered, the hushed whispers of the gathered mourners were like leaves rustling in a gentle breeze. The pews were lined with somber figures, their faces etched with the shared grief of Mikey's passing. The room was a tableau of sorrow, each person a brushstroke of loss in the larger portrait of Mikey's life.

The casket, a polished mahogany vessel, lay at the center of it all, a stark reminder of the finality that awaited us all. It was adorned with a spray of white roses, their petals a stark contrast to the dark wood, each one a silent ode to the friend we had lost. The air was laced with a melodic strain of a solemn dirge, the notes weaving through the space, wrapping around us like a comforting shroud.

As I approached the casket, the reality of the moment pressed down upon me. The coolness of the room seemed to seep into my bones, a physical manifestation of the cold truth that Mikey was no longer with us. The casket's lid was open, revealing Mikey's peaceful expression, as if he were merely in a deep slumber from which he might awaken at any moment.

Outside, the cemetery awaited, a tapestry of stone and marble that marked the resting places of countless souls. The procession moved like a slow river of black attire, winding its way through the rows of headstones. The sky wept a drizzle that kissed our cheeks, nature's own tribute to the boy who had touched so many lives.

At the graveside, the finality of the ceremony was palpable. The somber tones of the eulogy, the final prayers whispered into the chill air, and the soft thud of earth as it was cast upon the casket — each detail etched itself into my memory, a mosaic of the day we laid Mikey to rest.

One moment, you have someone with you, the other moment, they're gone. Just like that, it was almost like I imagined knowing him. Was this just a bad nightmare? Surely, it's time for me to wake up.

Chapter 5

Family Values

The world had narrowed to a series of losses — my best friend vanished, my sister confined, trust in my mother shattered, and the shelter's walls closing in. My life, a tapestry of misfortunes, seemed poised on the brink of unraveling. And on the precipice of this despair, my sixteenth birthday arrived, an uncelebrated milestone amidst the chaos.

There I was, amidst the cacophony of the shelter's youngest residents, when she appeared. "Kev, look what I've brought!" My mother's voice, bright with forced cheer, cut through the din. Her smile was a mask, hiding the strain of our strained bond.

I met her gaze, a fleeting connection that spoke volumes of the chasm between us. The children's laughter, innocent and carefree, underscored the silent tension that hung like a specter over us.

She had crafted a cake, a labor of love manifest in sugar and flour. It was the sort of confection that hinted at late-night efforts, at hands dusted with flour, at a heart yearning for absolution.

Her eyes lingered on me, a silent plea etched within their depths. I remained stoic, an island amidst her sea of regret. Yet, beneath my hardened exterior, a sliver of remorse stirred.

The cake, a sweet testament to her attempt at reconciliation, rested beside me. Its imperfect frosting mirrored the jagged edges of our relationship. I retreated to my corner, the sanctuary of my solitude, and there, I placed the cake upon my bed — a makeshift altar to her intentions.

The guilt that had been a mere whisper now roared to life, a crescendo of self-reproach. I found myself drawn to her room, compelled by an unseen force. The door creaked open to reveal her form, a silhouette of sorrow perched on the bed's edge.

"Thank you for the cake, Mom," I offered, the words heavy with unspoken apologies. Yet, they fell upon deaf ears, lost in the gulf of our mutual pain.

The silence that followed was a tangible entity, a bridge neither of us dared to cross. I turned to leave, the weight of our fractured past pressing down upon me. But her voice, a desperate whisper, halted me.

"Why do you harbor such anger, Kevin?" she implored. "Where have I erred so grievously?"

I stood, a tempest of emotions threatening to spill forth. Her continued pleas were a siren's call, luring the truth from its depths. "I question your efforts, Mom," I confessed, the dam of my restraint finally breaking. "True effort would not have surrendered Eve without a fight. A mother's instinct is to shield her children, yet you... you let her slip away. Is my fate to follow? Am I to be the next casualty of your ambitions?"

The release was cathartic, a purge of years of bottled fury. And as I witnessed the tears that finally breached her stoic facade, I understood the magnitude of my words. Her sobs, once muffled by night's embrace, now laid bare in the harsh light of day.

The years had been a mosaic of resentment towards my absent father, a silent battle between anger and the guilt of yearning for him. Yet, in the wake of the revelation, I found myself liberated from the need to conceal my love. The desire to blame my mother for our fractured lives clawed at me—a mother, a wife, who should have foreseen the fallout. But how could I sustain that bitterness? It was too late for hate.

She had erred, yes, but she had also endeavored to mend the broken threads of our family tapestry. She had been the constant in my nights of illness, the architect of our heart-to-heart dialogues that shaped my morals in the absence of a paternal model. Why she chose to unveil the truths she did, I may never comprehend. Perhaps it was my own pressing that cornered her into confession.

As she spoke, her words became a distant hum, uttering the unthinkable confession, one that made my heart ache, but also eased years of guilty longing, she revealed that she cheated on my father and that my sister Evelyn was my uncle Johnny's kid. Apparently, she was with my Uncle before, well what I thought was falling in love with my father, but as life would prove, nothing is what it seems and even my existence alone was a mere second best outcome, and during one of my father's absences to promote his music, was reminiscent of the country song called thunder roll... love lost... I have to be honest, I stopped listening to her sobbing confession. In a sense, I felt like like I was set free and my disappointment was overshadowed by the burgeoning fantasy of reuniting with my father. My mind wove dreams of shared moments — tossing a baseball under a Jersey sky, navigating the rites of driving, tending to the yard side by side. The tapestry of possibilities stretched out before me, vibrant and inviting.

Armed with the truth, I embraced a new quest: to seek out the man who was half of my origin. To bridge the chasm of years with the tentative steps of reacquaintance. This was my newfound purpose, my horizon to chase.

***

After spending a stretch in juvie, I figured Evelyn would've wisened up. You know, learned to zip it, keep her trap shut. But no, she remained the same old Evelyn—the kind of girl who could start a brawl in an empty room. And honestly, I'd grown accustomed to it. Maybe even relished it a little.

Fights? Yeah, they were my jam. Part of my DNA, etched into my skin like the ink on my arm.. Evelyn's knack for stirring up trouble? Well, that was just another flavor of chaos. I'd stopped being annoyed by it; instead, I found myself leaning into the adrenaline rush. Like a moth to a flame, I was drawn to those moments when fists met faces, when the world blurred into a frenzy of blows.

Now, let me clarify something: Evelyn wasn't just my sister. She was my cousin too, but that technicality didn't change a damn thing. We'd grown up side by side, like two weeds pushing through the same cracked pavement. A night of revelation — when the family secrets spilled out like cheap wine — wasn't about to rewrite years of shared history. Blood was blood, and our bond ran deeper than any whispered truth.

So there I was, strolling down the grimy alley, the neon glow of the streetlights casting jagged shadows. The usual suspects loitered—Quan, with his sneer, and the other two, their eyes sharp as switchblades. They sized me up, their gazes lingering on the ink that snaked up my forearm.

"What's that?" Quan jabbed a finger at my tattoo. "Your boyfriend's name, you sissy?!"

His buddies snickered, their laughter like broken glass. But I'd heard worse. Hell, I'd been called worse. So I squared my shoulders, ready to dish it back.

"Hey, Quan," I drawled, and before I could utter my comeback, one of the kids proceeded the verbal assault and said, "Check this out. This guy's a queer!"

The words hung in the air, a challenge flung like a gauntlet. But then Quan upped the ante, his grin twisted.

"Did he die from AIDS after you had gay sex with him?"

My vision blurred. Rage surged, a primal force that drowned out reason. I lunged, fists flying, and the world turned red. Blood sprayed, knuckles cracked, and somewhere in the chaos, Evelyn's voice cut through.

"Stop, Kevin! You're gonna kill him!"

I snapped out of it, blinking at the bloodied face of the first guy—the one who'd spat poison. The other two had bolted, leaving him crumpled on the pavement. I hesitated, my breath ragged, the taste of iron on my tongue.

We ran, Evelyn and I, our footsteps echoing off the alley walls. But I knew this wasn't over. Not by a long shot. The streets held grudges, and I had a family to protect—one way or the other. The night swallowed us whole, and I wondered which hole this twisted sibling bond would drag me into next.

Chapter 6

Fight or Flight

Evelyn and I bolted home, our breaths ragged, adrenaline still coursing through our veins. The front door swung open, and we stumbled inside, our secret etched in bruises and blood. Thank the stars, Mom wasn't here — she'd have a conniption if she saw us like this.

"Wash up before Mom gets back!" Evelyn's voice cracked, and she thrust a damp towel at me. I stood there, dazed, the cold fabric clinging to my face. What the hell had just happened?

"Quit standing there like an idiot!" Evelyn shoved me toward the bathroom, her eyes wide with panic. I scrubbed the blood off my knuckles, the water turning pink. She handed me a clean T-shirt, her fingers trembling.

This was new. Evelyn, feeling guilty? It was like spotting a unicorn at a rodeo. By the time Mom returned, we were patched up, our faces scrubbed clean. She breezed in, groceries in hand, her smile oblivious to the chaos we'd left behind.

"Oh, hello," she chirped, setting the bags down. "What a lovely surprise to have you both home early today."

We exchanged glances, our secret locked behind our teeth. Dinner was a stilted affair. Evelyn chattered, her words a smokescreen. Mom didn't notice the haunted look in my eyes, too busy ladling mac and cheese onto our plates. Evelyn's big mouth had its uses, after all.

I slipped away early, retreating to my narrow bed. The springs creaked as I lay there, staring at the ceiling. Sleep eluded me—the kid's blood on my hands, the taste of violence lingering. What if he died? What if we'd left him to bleed out on the pavement?

Jail. The word echoed in my mind. How long would I rot behind bars? And Mom—what would she say? Worse, Dad. The man who'd walked out on us, leaving a void that even my fists couldn't fill. I imagined meeting him, not as a screw-up with a rap sheet, but as someone he could be proud of.

The night stretched on, my thoughts spiraling down rabbit holes. The owl outside hooted, its eyes wide open, just like mine. Evelyn snored like a chainsaw, blissfully unaware.

Typical Evelyn. But for me, the darkness held no rest. Only questions, regrets, and the gnawing fear that our twisted sibling bond had just dragged me into a pit I might never climb out of.

The morning light filtered through the blinds, casting a fractured pattern on my bedroom floor. I blinked, disoriented, the remnants of a dream clinging to my consciousness like cobwebs. In that dream, I'd been pounding the kid from yesterday—each punch a release, a desperate attempt to erase the rage. But then, the impossible happened. My fist went right through him, and I fell into…what? A pool of blood? The memory blurred, like trying to grasp smoke.

Dad and Mikey—my two favorite people—floated in that crimson sea. Their faces were hazy, their eyes pleading. Excitement surged—I could reach them, touch them. But when I opened my mouth to call out, no sound emerged. Instead, I choked, the metallic taste of blood filling my mouth. Drowning. That's what it felt like. And then I woke up, gasping for air, my heart pounding against my ribs.

Strange how dreams can be both real and surreal. The residue clung to me, a whisper of something wicked. I sat on the edge of my bed, the sheets rough against my skin. Ten minutes passed—ten minutes of trying to shake off the unease. But it clung to me like a shadow.

"Kevin! Breakfast!" Mom's voice floated from the kitchen, barely two steps away. Our cramped shelter living space, we were in the second phase where you get a small apartment-like set up to prepare you for finally getting back on your feet—hardly deserving of the term "house"—was a testament to our struggles. Sixteen years old and still sharing a bedroom with Evelyn. Talk about being a loser. You could traverse the entire area within ten footsteps, if you dared.

"Coming!" I called back, pulling on a clean T-shirt. School awaited, a mundane escape from the chaos of home.

Evelyn, ever the instigator, lounged on her bed. "Rough night?" she teased, her eyes dancing. "Looks like someone didn't get much sleep."

"Ya, 'cause SOMEONE was snoring like a pig the whole night!"

"Hey!" Evelyn protested, her voice rising. "Mom! Aren't you gonna say anything?"

Classic Evelyn. Stir the pot, then drag someone else into the fray. As I headed to the kitchen, I wondered if my dream held any truth. If something wicked had indeed come our way, I hoped we were ready. Because in this cramped space, secrets festered, and our twisted sibling bond might be the only thing keeping us afloat. "Kevin, be nice to your sister," Mom's voice sliced through the morning haze, her concern as genuine as a thrift-store Rolex. But she had no clue how foul my mood really was.

"Ya, Kevin. Why are you in such a foul mood?" Evelyn chimed in, her smirk a neon sign flashing, "I've got your number." She'd replayed yesterday's incident in her mind, I could tell. But this wasn't the same Evelyn who'd panicked just a day ago. No, this was the Evelyn who reveled in chaos, who danced on the edge of danger like a moth drawn to a flame.

I rolled my eyes at her audacity. "Anyway, you guys are too old now to be starting such petty fights," Mom continued, her words a well-worn record. "Now, finish up your breakfast, and don't cause any trouble at school. I'm off then." She planted kisses on our heads, her love a fragile armor against the world.

Evelyn shoveled pancakes into her mouth, her nonchalance baffling. "How could you be so chill?" I asked, annoyance bubbling up like acid reflux.

"What do you think is gonna happen?" she shot back, her eyes daring me to unravel. "What are you so scared of? Take a chill pill."

"Take a fuckin' chill pill?!" My voice cracked. "That guy could be dead, Eve!"

"Oh, come on! He wasn't dead." Her certainty stopped me cold. Trust Evelyn to know a dead guy when she saw one. I stared at her, dumbfounded.

"Look," she leaned in, her voice low, "if anything, this will teach those idiots to actually respect you from now on. Out on the streets, respect is earned the hard way. Don't be scared to make a bitch bleed now and then. Keeps 'em in line."

And just like that, my twisted sister had handed me a playbook for survival. The streets were no place for soft hearts or trembling fists. Respect was a currency, and I was about to cash in. But as I watched Evelyn, her eyes gleaming with secrets, I wondered if this was a game we could ever win.

She talked like some mob boss. Her words, casual as a Sunday stroll, sliced through the air. "I thought about it last night, and really, we good. A little fear is good." She shoveled pancakes into her mouth, as if discussing the weather or the latest gossip. And you know what? Her nonchalance actually relaxed me. Maybe she was right— fear could be a weapon, a blade honed by experience.

The entire day at school, I felt untouchable. Like a gladiator stepping out of the arena, I strutted through the halls. Sure, I was paranoid. One of those guys was my senior, and my anxious mind concocted a hundred ways they could corner me—in the toilets, during lunch, or just about anywhere. But nothing happened. By the end of the school day, whatever was left of my anxiety had washed away like chalk in the rain.

But as always, Life's got this sneaky way of hitting you where it hurts when you're not looking. Walking home from school, I was on my own. Evelyn? She had her own stuff going on, probably hanging at some friend's place. The streets were the same as always, but you never know when they might turn on you. And bam—that's when it happened. A sharp crack on the back of my head, my ears ringing like they're on the fritz. My face was eating dirt before I knew it.

Took me a sec to get my eyes to work right, and there they were—the same jerks from yesterday. Minus the one I'd laid out, of course. One of them was swinging a baseball bat like he meant business. That thing must've been what hit me, because my head was pounding like crazy.

They were standing over me, looking all smug.

"You think you're hot stuff, huh?" Quan sneered.

"Little Roy's in the hospital 'cause of you, you jerk!" the other one added, and then—wham—a kick right to my side.

I grunted, pain shooting through me.

"Time to pay Roy a visit in the hospital, loser!" And another kick came flying in.

Man, I thought they were gonna end me right there.

I knew if I didn't do something fast, I'd be toast. But what could I do? They had me pinned down and caught off guard. Before I could even think, I was face-down, and they weren't about to let me up.

"Where's your trashy sister? We'll have fun with her after we're done with you," one of them said, and they both cracked up like it was the funniest thing ever.

That lit a fire under me. My survival switch flipped on. Adrenaline kicked in, and reason checked out. I don't know where the strength came from, but suddenly, I was all in, fighting like it was do or die. I grabbed their legs—those walking sticks of evil—and yanked them down to the pavement. My hands were scraped up, but who cares? It was fight back or fade out.

That was all the time I needed to get an upper hand on them. I scrambled up, my fingers closing around the baseball bat that had fallen by the punk's side. The wood was gnarled, unforgiving. I pressed it against the throat of one of the bastards until he passed out, his eyes rolling back like a slot machine hitting jackpot.

A few swings at the other guy, the bat connecting with bone and sinew. I didn't hold back. The world blurred—pain, rage, and the taste of blood, that familiar metallic taste. Then I ran. I swear I never ran so fast in my life. But no matter how fast I sprinted, their death threat echoed in my ears.

"Ya run on, white boy! How long you think you can keep runnin'? I'll kill you, bitch!" The words chased me, but it wasn't the threat that bothered me most. It was the label they slapped on me. I'm not even white, but that's how they saw me.

I didn't go home. Paranoia clung to me like a shadow. I couldn't risk leading them to Mom and Evelyn. So, I stayed at the park, huddled in the darkness, my breath ragged. By the time I heard Evelyn's voice, it was already dark.

"Kevin! There you are!" She grabbed my arm, and I winced. "I've been looking all around for you. Where the hell have you been?! Mom's worried sick. Come home now!"

Under the flickering lamppost, she scrutinized me, the uneven light casting my battered visage into stark relief. "Damn! You're a sight—like some creature from a nightmare. What in the world happened to you?"

Her words, though harsh, couldn't dampen the irony. "You," I said, a bitter laugh escaping me despite the pain.

"What the hell do you mean by that?"

"The guys from yesterday," I echoed her own words back to her, "They decided it was time for respect. Seems no one's keen on messing with us now." My tone was laced with sarcasm, a pointed reminder of her naivety. "You know, for someone who claims wisdom, you're awfully clueless."

She opened her mouth to protest, but I cut her off. "Enough, okay? Just stop. It's not safe for you here anymore. We need to get you home."

Her eyes, wide with concern, searched mine. "What's our next move?"

"Our move?" The idea seemed ludicrous. "There is no 'our' in this. You've played your part. Now, I need to handle what comes next. Just... stay out of it, please. And for once, just... try not to be the hero."

Anger and fear warred within me. The threats they had made against her echoed in my mind, a relentless torment. I couldn't stand idly by; action was the only course.

Upon returning home, my mother's shock was palpable. "Kevin, what has become of you?" Her voice trembled, a mix of fear and disbelief.

I chose silence as my refuge, a silent vow to protect what remained of my fractured world.

"Who did this? Just tell me the names." Mom's voice trembled, her maternal instincts aflame. She thought her little baby was getting bullied, that some teenage thugs had roughed me up. But the truth was far more dangerous, far more twisted. I couldn't tell her the whole story, so why tell her anything? I mean, I couldn't admit that I'd been going around getting into fights as a part-time activity. What would she even do? Call the police? And what good could they do?

"They'd ask me to identify the guys," I thought, "then dig into my activities, blame me to some extent. Keep on working the 'case,' and then what? In the meantime, while I'm busy hiding behind my mom, they can do anything once they know that I'm going to the police."

So, no, this had to be handled differently. Different than how Mom would handle it. I just walked straight to the bedroom, the weight of secrets heavy on my shoulders. "What is going on, Evelyn? I need to know!" Mom's voice followed me down the hallway, but I didn't turn back. The truth was a beast I couldn't tame, and I wondered how long I could keep it caged.

Did she ever call the school to find out? The question hung in the air, a fragile thread connecting past to present. But trust? That was a currency I'd spent long ago. Mom's words had become like faded billboards along the highway— promises that blurred into the landscape.

I never really trusted her word much after that. It was all a show, a script she recited to soothe her conscience. The role of a mother, the lines she had to say. But follow-through? That was optional.

Desperate to feel safe, I turned to the only way I knew. The dark alley beckoned, shadows swallowing my doubts. There they were—the guys who didn't belong in a white-collar neighborhood. Their very presence screamed "drug dealers."

"What ya lookin' for, kid?" The raspy voice cut through the night.

"A gun," I said, with no hesitation. The stakes were too high for second-guessing.

"Whoa, whoa, that ain't my drift. I just sell some Mary Jane. You interested?" His eyes held secrets, but I wasn't buying.

"No. Just tell me where I can get a gun."

"Go to Tony's Pizzeria," he said. "The guy running the joint might help you…if you can pay him."

Pay him. Well, that was going to be a bitch. But I'd figure it out. Installments, favors, whatever it took. I was determined to get a gun—the "how" was a puzzle I'd solve as I went.

So, I walked into that pizzeria, the scent of marinara and melted cheese wrapping around me like a warm hug. It was a slice of normalcy in a life that had taken a dark turn. But appearances could be deceiving. This wasn't just any pizza joint. The Italian guys huddled at the tables, their laughter echoing off the checkered walls. Authenticity, they said. But authenticity came with a price.

In those days, you could spell Kevin and Dumb the same way, and you wouldn't have been wrong. I was both—naive and desperate. The kind of dumb that led me here, chasing shadows in a place where pepperoni and secrets mingled.

Now that I was here, the neon glow of the sign outside casting a halo on the pavement, the next mission loomed. Ask someone to sell me a gun. The words tasted bitter, like overcooked crust. But this was survival, and I'd swallow anything to stay alive.

The pizza place looked so normal, the aroma of garlic knots and oregano masking the danger. Who do I even say it to? The waitress? The guy flipping pizzas? Or the cashier with a smile? It seemed ludicrous to ask for a Glock in a well-lit room, surrounded by families savoring their slices.

Maybe I could wait until closing time, slip a plea to the guy locking up. Safer that way. But as the lights blinked off, the shadows thickening, I approached the back door. Suddenly, everything went black.

I woke up with a black cloth over my head. The mesh allowed slivers of light, enough to see the outline of my predicament. "Boss, this fucker's up," a heavy voice cut through the darkness, thick with Italian accent. The room smelled of dough and danger. And I realized, I'd stepped into a world where pizza wasn't the only thing on the menu.

Then somebody patted my cheeks repeatedly, as if checking if I was still conscious. "Hey, fucker. Are you listening? Blink twice if yes." Their laughter echoed, a chorus of amusement. I counted about five men in the room by the distinct timbre of their laughs.

"That's enough, Marco. Let me see the little fucker." The big guy beside me removed the black cloth, and through squinted eyes, I saw a middle-aged Italian man. His gaze held questions, and I wondered how much he already knew.

"Why you being a creep around Tony's place, eh?" His voice was calm, but the room crackled with tension. "Don't you know whose joint this is? Who sent you? Eh?"

Who sent me? The blow to my head had scrambled my thoughts. "No one," I managed to reply, the words tasting like defeat.

"No one, eh? He says no one sent him." The room chuckled, an inside joke shared among them. "What were you doing around my property then? Do you just like to be a creep? Waiting for the ladies to pass by? Hoping to catch a glimpse under their skirts as the wind blows them up? Eh? Is that it?" His eyes bore into mine, dissecting my intentions.

Of course, they'd spotted me lurking around. Everything started to make sense. When you're someone as big as Tony, you have men on duty—watchful eyes scanning for suspicious characters like me. Before I could make it to the door, they grabbed me, dragged me to the back.

"No. I just wanted to buy a gun." The words hung in the air, a desperate plea. But in Tony's world, even desperation had a price.

"Say what now?" His amusement danced in the air, a waltz of curiosity.

"I want to buy a gun," I said, my voice firmer this time.

"A gun? For your school project?" The room chuckled, their laughter a backdrop to my desperation. But I wasn't here for a science fair exhibit.

"No. To protect my family." The words hung there, heavy as the truth. Tony's gaze bore into mine, assessing.

"Say no more, boy. You came to the right man. Familia comes above all, right? Untie him." His command echoed, and the big guy beside me followed suit.

As soon as my hands were free, I rubbed the back of my head. The bump throbbed, a reminder of my misadventures.

"I am Tony," he said, "I run things around here. Now, tell me, why do you need a gun, son?"

"My family's in danger," I replied, "I gotta do something about it. Some kids from the block are after me. They threatened to kill my sister too. I must protect her."

"Hmm. I see. See, boys. Now, this is something I respect. This is what our youth lacks. Our young men oughta be more like you,…. ? ."

He paused, waiting for my name.

"Kevin. Kevin V. Turner." I replied

"Alright then, Kevin, my boy. What kinda gun do you want?" Tony's voice held a mix of curiosity and authority. I'd stepped into a world where choices had consequences, and this was no ordinary shopping trip.

"I dunno, something that does the job and isn't too heavy duty." My words felt small in the cavernous room, but Tony seemed to understand.

"Oh, I got just the thing." He disappeared into the shadows, reemerging with an antique pistol. "Don't go on its size, this little gal's a killing machine. Here," he placed the weapon in my hand, "feel her. Makes you feel powerful, doesn't it?"

I nodded, my fingers tracing the cold metal. This was my first time holding a real gun. "How much is it?" I asked, meekly aware of my empty pockets.

74

"Don't you worry about that, my boy! Your goal is respectable, and I want to support it. That's what I do for little boys here: turn them into men. You take this now and don't worry about a thing, ok?" His kindness felt like a lifeline, but I didn't realize it was all part of his grand plan. I just nodded, left with the gun in my pocket, and stepped out into the night.

I felt invincible. The weight of the weapon pressed against my hip, a promise and a curse.

Chapter 7

Kevin's Got a Gun

I kept feeling the gun in my pocket all the way home, its weight a secret I carried. Like a kid with Halloween candy, I clung to the promise of power. Now that I had what I needed, the next step loomed—a dance with fate. I wouldn't make the same mistake twice. I had to strike before they jumped me again, before their fists found my face, before their threats reached my sister's ears.

So I decided to bring the gun to school, to settle the score in the fluorescent-lit corridors. I planned it out meticulously, the locker rooms my chosen battleground. When everyone cleared out, I'd corner the guy who'd threatened me, hold him at gunpoint, and vanish into the shadows. Sounds solid enough, right? For a 16-year-old, yes. But I hadn't factored in the acoustics of fear—the way gunshots echoed, the way silence screamed.

Feeling confident and powerful, I followed through on my plan. I spotted the group of guys, tailed them into the locker room. My heart raced as I cornered the dude, my finger trembling on the trigger. But then he spotted me, his eyes widening. "Hey, you!" His voice cut through the steam, "What the fuck you doing here? I knew this guy was gay, man! Look at him sneaking in the showers!"

The whole room turned, their laughter a tidal wave. So much for my perfect planning. The gun in my pocket felt like a curse, and I wondered if I'd just stepped into a trap of my own making.

The embarrassment rushed to my head. The locker room had become a stage, and I was the unwitting actor in a tragicomedy. To save myself from it, I pulled out the gun— the cold metal a talisman against humiliation. Everyone gasped in unison, their eyes wide, their laughter silenced.

"Whoa, man! I don't know what's going on here," another guy stammered, "but ya'll's gotta cool it, ok?" He edged away, hands raised in surrender. I pointed the gun at him in panic, and he retreated further. "This is what happens when you fuck around too much," I muttered, my finger trembling on the trigger.

Nothing. The gun remained silent, a prop in my desperate play. I pulled the trigger again and again, then hit it like our old TV remote—a percussive plea for functionality. The room erupted in laughter, and I felt so stupid, so out of my depth.

Before I could run out, the coach tackled me to the ground. Talk about perfect timing. His weight pressed me into the linoleum, and I wondered if this was my punishment for playing with fire.

"What is going on here?" His voice cut through the chaos, and we all looked at him, confused, wondering what do we even say.

The next thing I knew, I was sitting in the principal's office, my mom's fury a tempest. I was expelled from school. The words hung there, a sentence etched in shame. I would have been arrested, if it hadn't been for the "Prop Gun" etched on the side of the weapon. "Where the hell did you even get that thing from? What were you even thinking? What if it was real? What was your plan?" My mom's voice was a storm, and I had no answers. Only regrets.

"Murderer? Is that what I've raised?" The accusation hung in the air, a shroud of disbelief and horror.

"You come home with your face marred by violence, and you expect me to remain silent? What in God's name is happening to you, Kevin?" My mother's voice was a crescendo of fear and confusion as we stepped through the threshold of what was once a sanctuary. I had no words to offer, no salve for the wounds that weren't visible. Her eyes, once filled with warmth, now bore into me with cold resolve.

"If you refuse to confide in me, then you have no place here. I cannot harbor a stranger, especially one cloaked in danger." Her declaration was a gavel's fall, and with it, I was rendered homeless. With a heart heavy as lead, I gathered my meager belongings and sought refuge in the only other place I knew—Tony's domain.

"You handed me a weapon of deceit!" I confronted him, the betrayal stinging like a fresh wound.

"Deceit?" Tony's laugh was a baritone rumble, his amusement as clear as the disbelief in his eyes. "That piece is as genuine as Tina's charms," he quipped, nodding towards the waitress who bore her enhancements with a resigned eye-roll. His cronies chuckled, their mirth echoing off the pizzeria's walls.

"It failed to fire!" I protested, the frustration evident in my voice.

"And what price did you pay for it? Remind me," he teased, his laughter a second blow.

"I paid nothing—"

"Exactly!" Tony cut me off. "In this life, you get what you pay for, and nothing comes without a cost. Understand?" The realization dawned on me; I was a pawn in his game, a disposable piece in his grand design. Perhaps he had anticipated this outcome, or worse, hoped I'd fall and fade into oblivion. Either way, Tony stood to gain. "If it's sanctuary you seek, I can provide it," he offered, a sly glint in his eye. "How? I'm adrift, Tony. My own mother has cast me out. I have nowhere to turn," I pleaded, the desperation raw in my voice. "Calm down, kid. I have a place for you, just above this very shop. Work for me, and it's yours." His offer, laced with generosity, was a lifeline I couldn't afford to question. With no other options, I accepted, stepping into the unknown.

Months later, I realized that meeting Tony was the best thing that happened to me. I was protected and respected. Tony wasn't just The Neighborhood Pizza Guy; he was a force of nature. A big middle-aged Italian guy, about 270 pounds, with a slicked-back haircut and a tight fade. His shirts always seemed a bit too small, straining against his broad chest. The soiled apron around his waist told stories of countless pizzas crafted, secrets whispered over dough and sauce. And that unlit cigar, perpetually clenched between his teeth, was both a prop and a statement.

The back table of the pizzeria was Tony's throne. The plate of pizza crust, a ritual. The glass with the bottle of single-barrel scotch, a mystery. I'd asked him once why he kept the glass if he never used it. "I'm working on my figure," he'd said, "gotta stay away from the extra carbs."

Tony's world was a blend of flour and fire, secrets and simmering sauces. And as I settled into the little apartment above the shop, I realized that I'd stepped into more than a place to stay. I'd entered Tony's orbit, where protection came with a price, and respect was earned in slices.

Tony's mentorship had become a cornerstone of my existence, his words a creed etched into the fabric of my daily life. "You never hurt a guy that doesn't deserve it," he'd say, or "Shoot first, die last." These were not just phrases; they were the laws of survival in a world where hesitation could mean the difference between life and death.

The modest one-bedroom above the pizzeria was no palace, but it was a sanctuary compared to the cold, unforgiving streets. I found solace in the simple tasks Tony assigned me—wiping tables, fetching cheese, making deliveries. They were small ways to repay the debt of gratitude I owed him for pulling me from the brink.

But the job evolved, and the pizza deliveries soon became a front for something more. That day, as I stepped into the shop, Tony's gaze held a new intensity. "Kid, you know you're like a son to me, right?" His question hung in the air, heavy with unspoken meaning.

"Um, thanks, man, I appreciate you," I managed, fumbling with the weight of his words. It was the best response I could muster, a feeble attempt to acknowledge the bond he claimed.

"I want to let you in on a little extra money if you're interested," he continued. In my world, more money equated to fewer problems. It was an offer that, despite the risks, I couldn't afford to refuse.

In the dimly lit back room of Tony's pizzeria, where the scent of marinara clung to the air like a guilty secret, I stood face-to-face with my fate. Tony, the big middle-aged Italian guy who'd taken me under his wing, leaned against the flour-dusted counter. His slicked-back hair and tight-fitting shirt gave him an air of authority, but it was his eyes—the kind that had seen too much—that held my attention.

"You might not remember," Tony began, "but when you were about eight, I watched you kick this kid's ass up and down the street. Man, you had a mean left hook." Memories stirred—the taste of victory, the sting of knuckles meeting flesh.

"Yeah, you can thank my sister for that," I replied, a nod to Evelyn's vicious mouth that forged my fists.

Tony chuckled, "You got heart, kid, and that's what I'm looking for." His words hung there, a bridge between loyalty and obligation.

But then he shifted gears, his gaze sharpening. "I got a few more guys that owe me a little change," he said, "and well, I just want you to take care of them for me." The proposition hung in the air, heavy as the Louisville slugger he tossed my way. You give a quick swing of the bat," Tony continued, "and always swing with bad intentions. Bring me my money; you got it, kid!"

"You think you could do it, boy?" His eyes bore into mine, years ahead of my experience. "You wanna do this one? You think you can go and get the money from Rocco?"

I'd never done anything like that, but I knew hesitation was a luxury I couldn't afford. If I blew this chance, Tony wouldn't ask me again. Maybe he would; knowing him, he liked to exploit young blood. Get these jobs done in less by grooming clueless idiots like me.

I was desperate to prove myself, and with all eyes on me, I felt like if I said no or even asked how, they'd think I'm a pussy. I'd rather die than let that be my position. So, without further thinking, I just said, all cool and collected, "Ya, I can do that.

Tony looked mildly impressed, his eyes lingering on me as if measuring my resolve. Maybe after my dumbass move of getting a fake gun from him, he'd underestimated me. But now, standing in the dimly lit alley, I was about to prove myself—or die trying.

"You know the drill," Tony's voice was gravel and shadows. "Just go up to the address I give and say, 'Tony sent me.' Not a word more, not a word less. Capeesh? Don't try to be a smartass, boy. I don't like smartasses."

I nodded, my heart drumming against my ribs. I went as instructed, the words rehearsed on my tongue. Not much was needed to say—just those three syllables: "Tony sent me." The streets had their own language, and everyone understood the code.

Never a hiccup, until that one time when a guy tried to be a smartass. I walked up to him, the words poised on my lips. "Tony sent me," I said, my voice steady.

The guy just looked at me, his eyes assessing. "So?" His voice was a challenge, a dare. I was confused, my mind racing. I couldn't say anything, just stood there, dumbfounded.

I knew if I started swinging, I could take this man. But he was on his turf, surrounded by at least ten of his men, and knowing how things worked in the streets, ten more could come within the first five minutes of the fight. I wasn't stupid. So I did what I was instructed: "Not a word more."

I didn't say any more, just left and went back to the pizzeria, to give Tony the rundown.

"He said what?" Tony's incredulity was palpable, his voice a low growl of disbelief.

I repeated the man's words, the absurdity of the situation hanging between us.

"This guy's unhinged," Tony muttered. "Marco, deal with this." And just like that, the matter was settled. Marco, along with two others and myself, returned to the address. What transpired there was a brutal display of power—a violent reimagining that left an indelible mark on my conscience.

I've weathered many brawls, but nothing could have prepared me for the ferocity of that night.

Reflecting on my initial foray into this shadowy world, I confess my trepidation was palpable; my legs trembled as though I'd endured a grueling race. The dry cleaner's on North 28th Street was my first stop, and I had naively anticipated a modest haul—mere pocket change. Yet, what I encountered was a staggering sum, a fortune that far exceeded any expectations. The collections were typically straightforward, but occasionally, a defiant soul would challenge the status quo. As Tony advised, a decisive swing of the bat was all it took to resolve any disputes. Before long, my mere presence was enough to ensure the swift surrender of money, no questions asked.

My reputation preceded me, whispered on the lips of every streetwise figure; my name echoed through the alleys and shops all throughout the city, as Tony said he makes boy men and I was learning what that meant.

Tony's weekly kickback of $500 was a fortune in my world, a sum that dwarfed any amount I'd ever laid eyes on. One day, curiosity overcame me, and I dared to question the source of this wealth. Tony's gaze met mine, a mix of amusement and warning dancing in his eyes.

"Kid, if I tell you, I'll have to kill you," he jested, before his expression sobered. "No, seriously, don't ask me any more dumb questions. Just do your job. You got it, kid?"

His words, meant to be light-hearted, sent a shiver down my spine. I laughed, a hollow sound, as a knot formed in my throat. Tony's demeanor shifted, perhaps sensing my unease. "Hey kid, back in Sicily, where I'm from, you don't pry into matters that don't concern you," he advised. His words sent my world spinning, the walls closing in, my pulse skyrocketing, and a clammy sweat breaking out. A cacophony of ringing filled my ears—a harbinger of the panic attacks that would soon become all too familiar.

Once I got the hang of it and settled into my new role, I felt invincible. If anybody tried to be a smartass, I knew how to deal with it and put the fear of God—or, should I say, the fear of Tony—in them. It was hard to know when Tony was joking. That was the thing with people like him; you could never trust them because, in a way, they never trusted anyone either. Trust was a two-way street. If you didn't trust someone, no one could completely trust you. You had to give in to some extent first. Let the other person in. And when you were in the kind of business Tony was, you couldn't afford to make that mistake.

So even though, with time, I saw that he started to put some trust in me, and I began to take his word for many things too, I could still sense that neither he nor I would count on each other on a bad day. We were both survivors, playing a dangerous game where loyalty was a currency that could be devalued at any moment. Eventually, he let me in on his real business, drug dealing and I was locked into his world like a prisoner, but life was good and I played my role,

I was among the top drug lords in the city, living the high life. Luxury cars, expensive jewelry, luxury hotel penthouse living—you name it. Evelyn was doing better, and Mom had finished her program, finding a small apartment in a safer neighborhood. Life was good, or at least as good as it could be in this twisted underworld. But there was always a price to pay, and the shadows cast by my choices were growing longer.

The rift between my mother and me had grown into a chasm since the day she cast me out. Not once had she spoken my name to Evelyn or inquired about my well-being. In hindsight, my stubbornness seems petty, a needless prolongation of conflict. Yet, at the time, it felt justified.

Tony's world was one of unfathomable wealth, a realm where I managed to carve out a semblance of success despite the odds. But beneath the veneer of prosperity, a void lingered within me. The power and riches at my fingertips did little to quell the sense that my existence was meant for something more profound. I had strayed from my path and now faced the daunting task of finding my way back.

High school lessons on the nature versus nurture debate echoed in my mind, an unresolved discourse on the roots of morality. But life had taught me that survival is the crucible that forges character. It tests the mettle of both your innate disposition and your upbringing. My mother's nurturing never hinted at a future entangled with the underworld, yet here I stood, a drug dealer by circumstance. Was this latent within me all along? I think not, or else I wouldn't feel so out of place, an aberration amidst the pizzeria's patrons who seemed born for this life.

Perhaps among them were souls like mine, swept away by life's cruel currents, trapped in a relentless struggle for survival. Along the way, something within me shifted; survival mode became my constant state.

It's peculiar how our youthful dreams seldom align with reality's twists. Had someone told a six-year-old me that my family would crumble, that homelessness and crime would mark my journey, I would have dismissed them as mad. Yet, here I am, their prophecy fulfilled. As a child, I clung to idyllic visions of a perfect existence—a harmonious household where love and laughter were ever-present. Now, I grapple with the fragments of that dream, seeking to piece together a new vision from the shards of a fractured past.

In the dim glow of streetlights, I pondered the imperfections of life, the realization dawning on me that perfection was a myth, and existence was the art we crafted from our choices. It was a canvas I had painted with my own hands, yet a nagging sensation whispered that this path was not my destiny. No matter the depth of my immersion or the proficiency I achieved, it felt as if the heavens themselves had parted to acknowledge my presence, a celestial voice calling out, "Kevin, you are seen," amidst the mundane backdrop of my return to the pizzeria, where I performed tasks for Tony—tasks he deemed just, a settling of debts. But in moments of clarity, I suspected that some of those ensnared owed nothing to the shadows of the underworld.

Resuming my tale, I recall the night's chill as I made my way back to the shop, the hum of an engine tailing me. Tony's influence ran deep, and 'Pimpinella' was our safeguard—a whimsical twist on a fairytale name that could transform a police encounter into a contrite retreat. Yet, this encounter diverged from the routine. A veiled SUV trailed me, and upon halting, a figure emerged to approach my car. The window lowered, and an envelope landed in my lap, its contents declaring an inheritance decreed by NY statute and section 413 of the minor estate law, a legacy bequeathed by Clevland Turner, to be claimed upon my eighteenth year, accompanied by a handwritten missive from my father. As swiftly as he appeared, the messenger vanished, the SUV fleeing the scene with the urgency of a crime.

That night, the letter became an object of my fixation, turning over in my hands as I sat on the brink of my bed, wrestling with a torrent of questions. Could this be reality? Who was this enigmatic courier? My father's whereabouts remained a mystery, and the burning question lingered— why had he not come in person? The envelope, a bearer of truths and uncertainties, lay before me, an invitation to a destiny yet unwritten.

Questions swirled around me, a tempest of doubt and fear, as I held the enigmatic letter. It was a Pandora's box in parchment, promising answers yet threatening to unleash more chaos into my already tumultuous existence. I hesitated, fearing that its contents might ignite the kindling of questions within me, leaving me more lost than before.

Dawn broke with a vengeance, its light a stark contrast to the scant hours of restless slumber I had managed. The letter, a silent sentinel on my nightstand, stood as a testament to the reality of the previous night's events. It was a beacon, urging me to confront the unknown. My phone shattered the morning stillness, its shrill tone a drill sergeant in the quiet of my room. Annoyed, I answered gruffly, "Who is this?"

"Mr. Turner?" The voice on the other end was a calm oasis in my storm of irritation.

"Yes, who's this?"

"I represent your father, Cleveland Turner," came the reply, professional and detached.

The fog of sleep lifted instantly.

"We hope the letter was delivered to you last evening."

"Yeah, it was practically thrown at me."

"Please, when you're ready, let's discuss the details. There are legalities to be addressed."

"Alright," I responded, my voice heavy with the weight of unanswered questions. I hung up, my mind a whirlwind. Was this some elaborate ruse? A scene from a film playing out in my life?

I reached for the letter, its presence now a siren call to action. As my fingers grazed the seal, the phone interrupted once more. Tony's name flashed on the screen. "Where are you, kid?" His voice was a snarl through the speaker. "It's way past your time. This isn't a game. Get here in ten, or there'll be hell to pay." The urgency in his tone was the jolt I needed. The letter would have to wait. Duty called, and I answered.

Chapter 8

When the Levee Breaks

The day unfolded like any other, with the usual demands and the facade of toughness I've perfected. Yet, today was different; my thoughts were ensnared by the morning's call and the letter that lay unopened. My mind wandered, painting portraits of a father I had never known. Would he see himself in me? Did we share any common ground? The thought of playing catch, a simple act so foreign to me, lingered with a tinge of hope. Fatherhood was an abstract concept, a role I had never seen modeled.

The evening brought me back to my apartment, a sanctuary from the day's masquerade. I reached for the phone, the number burning in my memory. The line connected, and the familiar voice of Brookes and Associates greeted me. "I need to speak with my father," I said, a mix of anticipation and dread in my voice.

The pause that followed was laden with an unspoken truth. "I'm sorry, that's not possible," the voice replied, a note of reluctance in the air. Frustration flared within me. "Why not?"

The answer came like a blow, cold and unforgiving. "Your father passed away in a plane crash two weeks ago." The words echoed, a cruel twist to a story I had only just begun to piece together. The man I had envisioned meeting all my life, the enigmatic figure who had occupied my thoughts, was gone.

The voice continued, detailing an inheritance that felt like a hollow consolation. Turner Productions, a legacy awaiting my eighteenth birthday, a fortune that now seemed like an empty gesture. I cut the call short, the legalities meaningless in the face of loss.

Alone with the letter, I hesitated, the weight of the heavy paper in my hands. It was a tangible connection to a man who had remained an enigma, his choices now etched in ink. The rhythm of his writing, the pressure of the pen, the hurried splatters—all spoke of urgency, of words that needed to be freed before doubt could take hold.

The handwriting, jagged and bold, mirrored my own. It was a genetic echo, a reminder of how traits and quirks are woven through the tapestry of our lineage. In that moment, the letter was more than paper; it was a bridge to the past, a link to the man whose blood coursed through my veins.

It was brief, the message succinct, yet it resonated with a clarity that only a father's words could convey. Perhaps he knew, in his final moments, what his son needed to hear.

I love you, son, and I'm sorry I couldn't be there for you. If you're reading this, I guess something happened to me, and as instructed, Brooke's and Associates would have found you by now. I know you have questions; just know I never forgot about you. I was homeless for a while after I moved out and finally got a record deal and back-pay for a few records that I didn't get royalties on. Put it this way: everything I worked for is yours. I stopped by our old house to let you know I was filing for custody. I guess your mom moved you guys somewhere. I worked hard and I felt like I would never get my big break, but God is good. Son, always remember it's never too late to do the right thing and don't be mad at your mom. I was always faithful, but my dreams got in the way, I guess I'm writing this just in case I don't see you again and most importantly, lil' man, there's something I want you to know is that the day has come, and you are better than me.

Love, Dad

Tears had become strangers to me, absent through countless beatings and the day my mother's door closed behind me. Yet, in a solitary moment, they returned, cascading like a deluge of long-suppressed grief. I wept for the father who became a ghost of promises, for the childhood dreams that dissolved into the ether, for the questions that would forever echo unanswered. It was a catharsis I hadn't known I needed.

Time marched on, and the man from the law firm faded from my thoughts. Eighteen loomed on the horizon, a beacon of independence, but my focus lay elsewhere. I was entrenched in the hustle, the relentless pursuit of my own legacy. Yet, a part of me yearned to abandon this path, to fulfill the aspirations of a younger Kevin—to reunite my family, to absolve my mother's guilt, to offer Evelyn a life unmarred by the stains of my choices.

Now, I found myself a king of a tarnished crown, indebted to Tony, pockets lined with cash, surrounded by a sea of faces devoid of meaning. My Friday nights had become a tableau of excess and escape, a gathering of souls lost in the haze of their own despair. In their company, I found a perverse solace, a reflection of my own desolation.

Alone in the penthouse that towered over the city's decay, I retreated into the sanctum of the master suite. The letter from my father, worn from the countless times I'd unfolded its creases, brought him back to me in whispers of ink and paper. "I love you, son, and I'm sorry I couldn't be there for you…" The words seared into my being, a brand of sorrow and love intertwined. "…the day has come, and you are better than me. Love, Dad."

The letter, a tangible piece of a man I longed to know, was all that remained. It bore the weight of a $15.2 million legacy within Turner Productions—a fortune I would relinquish without a second thought for a moment in his presence. As sleep claimed me, I dared to dream of a world where perfection was within reach, where the fractures of my life would mend. I drifted off, cradling the belief that I could right the wrongs, that I could piece together the fragments of a dream once cherished. I must have fallen asleep reading my father's letter for the hundredth time and I woke up to a living hell, my worst nightmare.

The hotel penthouse was desolate, a stark reminder of the night's betrayal. I had been robbed of everything—money, drugs, and perhaps my future. The looming threat of Tony's wrath was palpable; the man had a reputation for making examples out of those who crossed him. Yet, there was a sliver of hope—if I could reach him before the rumors did, maybe I could negotiate my way out.

Approaching Tony's pizzeria, I was a bundle of nerves. This was the man who had been a father figure to me, albeit a harsh one. I clung to the hope that beneath his tough exterior, there might be a hint of understanding. The sight of him, cigar in hand, scotch at the ready, and surrounded by discarded pizza crusts, was oddly comforting.

I mustered the courage to speak, but Tony's reaction was swift and brutal. The chokehold, the elbow to the gut—it was a clear message. Yet, he spared me, a gesture that spoke volumes. His bear hug and whispered words were a mix of threat and reprieve. I had two months and one final job.

As I stumbled out into the cold New York air, the realization hit me—I was homeless again. But this time, it was different. I had an inheritance coming, a chance to start anew. The hardships I faced now would soon be a distant memory. I would have the means to right the wrongs, to build the life I had always dreamed of—a life where my family would never want for anything.

The future was uncertain, but one thing was clear: I was on the brink of change, and I was ready to embrace it, whatever it may take.

The streets have a way of teaching hard lessons, and as I found myself without a roof for the second time, the reality of my choices weighed heavily on me. The first day back in the clutches of homelessness was a brutal reminder of the life I had left behind—a life filled with warmth, love, and the simple joys of family. The memory of my mother's baking and my father's music was a stark contrast to the biting cold and gnawing hunger I faced.

As I nestled between two strangers around a barrel fire, the flames flickered like the ghosts of my past, conjuring up images of a time when my biggest concern was who would rap first—me or my dad. Those were the days of dreams and aspirations, where the future was a stage waiting for us to claim it. But reality has a way of intruding, and soon enough, the complexities of adult relationships and the harsh truths of my family's history came crashing down.

The revelation of my mother's affair with my uncle, the tangled web of love and betrayal, was a burden I carried with me. It was a story of human frailty, of dreams deferred, and of the messy, imperfect nature of life. The alleyway, with its transient warmth and the company of souls as lost as I, became a refuge from the storm of my thoughts.

Each night, as I unfolded the letter from my father, I clung to the promise of a better tomorrow—a future where the weight of $15 million would lift me from the depths of despair. I held onto hope for my mother, for Evelyn, and for myself. The streets may have been my present, but they would not define my future. And as the saying goes, be careful what you wish for—because sometimes, wishes do come true, in ways we least expect.

Chapter 9

The Depths of Desperation

As the dawn of my eighteenth year approached, it loomed not with the promise of freedom, but with the shadow of a debt I owed to Tony—a debt that threatened to cost me more than money. The sum of $45,000 hung over me like a guillotine, poised to sever me from the life I clung to. Desperation clawed at my mind, seeking an escape, a solution, anything.

It was during one of my aimless wanderings, a routine I had perfected in my days of destitution, that providence cast its peculiar light upon me. The business section of the Hudson Newspaper fluttered into my path, its headlines screaming of success and dreams realized. "Local entrepreneur's culinary venture becomes the talk of the town," it proclaimed. Sandra T's Deli and Cafe, the article boasted, had become an overnight sensation. And there, nestled among the accolades, a personal touch: "Try Kevin's favorite cookie." My mother, against all odds, had achieved her dream. Pride swelled within me, tempered by the ache of longing. I yearned to see her, to share in her triumph, but the timing was all wrong. I needed to rid myself of Tony's shadow first, to piece my life back together.

My reverie was shattered by the purr of an engine—a black Lexus, sleek and foreboding, pulling up beside me. Tony emerged from the depths of luxury, his presence a stark contrast to my own. The window descended slowly, revealing a glimpse of a fortune that mocked my predicament. "I want my money, kid," he sneered, his gaze dripping with disdain. "And by the looks of it, you're coming up short. Better start hustling if you want to keep breathing." With a flick of his wrist, he tossed a crumpled hundred-dollar bill at my feet—a taunt, a reminder of my debt—as he drove away.

The money burned in my pocket, but it bought me a momentary respite—a hot meal, a semblance of normalcy. It was then that the plan, dark and desperate, took root in my mind. I would rob Sandra T's Deli and Cafe. My mother would never suspect her own son, and I was certain the day's earnings were there for the taking. The thought of betraying her trust was a bitter pill to swallow, but the alternative was a fate far worse under Tony's heel.

I steeled myself, gazing into the fractured reflection of a shop window. The person staring back was a stranger, a shadow of the boy I once was. For the first time, I recoiled from my own image, from the path I was about to tread. But there was no turning back.

With a breath that tasted of desperation, I pushed through the doors of the deli, my resolve hardening with each step. I didn't hesitate, didn't falter. I pressed a candy bar against my mother's back, a silent threat that spoke volumes. She didn't panic—she never did. She was the rock that had anchored me through the storms of life, the steady hand that guided me when our world fell apart.

She filled my bag with the day's takings, and I fled, the weight of the money heavy in my hands. But as I made my escape, a piece of me was left behind—my sleeve caught on the door, revealing the ink that marked my skin. "Kevin!" my mother's voice pierced the air, a single word that carried the weight of realization, of heartbreak.

I ran, the streets blurring around me, until I found a quiet corner to count the spoils. $60,000—more than enough to settle my debt with Tony. Relief washed over me, chased quickly by a tide of guilt. Her voice haunted me, a siren call that begged the question: Should I turn back? Should I face the consequences of my actions?

The decision lay heavy on my soul, a crossroads between redemption and ruin.

Chapter 10

The Final Job

The relentless march of time brought me to Tony's doorstep once more, my heart a tumult of emotions. I laid the fruits of my betrayal before him, a sum that should have freed me from his clutches. Yet, as he cast his sinister gaze upon the money, I felt the ground beneath me shift. With a smirk that chilled my blood, Tony dismissed my offering with a flick of his wrist, consigning the cash to the flames of his pizza oven. The sight of currency turning to ash was a stark reminder of the world I was trapped in—a world where life's value was measured by loyalty to men like Tony.

His words were a slap to my already battered conscience. "You just don't get it, do you, kid?" he taunted, his voice a venomous hiss. "I didn't want you here till next week. What kind of fool are you?" His threat was clear: one last job, or else. The money was nothing but a casualty in his game—a game played under the watchful eyes of the law, a game where he was always one step ahead.

I fled, the echo of his threats ringing in my ears, the weight of my choices heavy on my soul. The city streets offered no solace, no refuge from the storm that raged within me. Thoughts of turning to the authorities danced in my mind, a fleeting hope quickly extinguished by the reality of Tony's reach. He was a shadow that stretched far and wide, a darkness that not even the law could illuminate.

Days blurred into one another, each passing moment drawing me closer to the inevitable—the final job, the last act in Tony's twisted play. And as fate would have it, the curtain would rise on this final scene just as I stood on the threshold of adulthood.

I entered the shop, the familiar scent of dough and sauce a stark contrast to the tension that filled the air. Tony, usually a storm cloud of fury, greeted me with an unsettling warmth. He offered me a seat, a drink, a slice—courtesies never extended before. It was a gesture that reeked of finality, of endings.

He laid out the tools of my last task with the care of a craftsman—a small black duffle bag filled with instruments of violence and control. Fishing hooks, a crowbar, a machete, a 9mm with two clips, and a length of rope. Each item, a silent testament to the gravity of what lay ahead.

As I stared at the contents of the bag, a realization settled over me. This was more than a job; it was a test—a test of will, of morality, of the very essence of who I was. Would I become the monster Tony saw in me, or would I find the strength to break free from the chains he had wrapped so tightly around my life?

The choice was mine, and mine alone.

"Do you know of the Zigerelli family in Jersey? The governor?" he probed. It appeared they had attempted to sacrifice me to save their own skin. But I'm always one step ahead. Surely, you didn't believe the robbery was mere happenstance? The last complication I needed was your untimely arrival, threatening to unravel my empire. You see, I am the linchpin here, the wealthiest man in the metropolis. Yet, you emerged, a naive youth with grandiose aspirations, believing the world owed you a life of opulence. But from birth, the world promises us nothing but the inevitability of death, and that debt is paid by all. Now, you play a pivotal role. I need you to handle the Zigerelli matter."

I was stunned. The audacity to have his own stash pilfered? It was almost laughable. And who else but Tony could be the target of such folly? Once more, I was his pawn. Yet, I was in no position to object.

I inquired about the task, "What exactly do you mean by 'handle them'?"

"I expect you to deliver their due: eliminate them. Choose any instrument from this bag, and if you falter, I will ensure you experience a fate far worse. Is my message crystal clear, boy?" He flung his Lexus keys at me. "Make it so, and let this be our final exchange. Agreed?"

I could only nod. My options were nonexistent. Clutching the bag, I staggered to the car, bile rising in my throat. The notion of taking a life was too much to bear. The bag's contents were sinister, each tool as daunting as the next. Composing myself, I slid into the driver's seat and set off towards the Lincoln Tunnel, my mind awash with memories of better days. Memories of Evelyn, crafting forts beneath the kitchen table, listening intently to tales of a time before her existence, filled my thoughts. I clung to the hope that our father might return to us. She never grasped why I bothered to speak of him; to her, he was merely a name on a birth certificate. I cherished those early morning and late-night conversations with my mother, envisioning a future for our family, her unwavering belief that we would persevere, even when life led us to a shelter. She held onto hope, a sentiment Evelyn seemed to have misplaced, or perhaps she simply learned to cope differently.

The remainder of the journey passed in a haze. My body had succumbed to numbness, perspiration drenched my skin. I had made my share of reckless decisions, but taking a life was a boundary I was reluctant to cross. Yet, the stark choice before me—them or myself—yielded a grim resolution. With newfound resolve, I parked outside the gated enclave of multimillion-dollar homes, scaled the fence, and navigated to the rear of the Zigerelli's sprawling estate. Defiantly, I settled on the firearm as my means of escape from this predicament. Surveying the grounds, I plotted potential hiding spots, resolving that the empty swimming pool would serve as an unlikely refuge should the need arise. With cautious steps, I approached the back entrance.

The Zigerelli residence was ablaze with light, the back door yielding to a gentle push, releasing a swell of old-world Italian melodies and the comforting aroma of garlic bread and simmering marinara. I navigated through the kitchen, the dining area coming into view. The thought of violence at the family dinner table was abhorrent, yet resolve steeled my nerves. I edged closer, the family's silhouettes within reach.

A moment of panic—my hand grasped at an empty waistband. The gun, forgotten in the car. As I cursed my oversight, a chilling realization set in: the family had already met their fate, executed by another's hand. My heart seized as I spun around, only to be met with the cold kiss of a pistol against my cheek. Tony's voice, laced with menace, whispered, "You never understood, did you? Live by the sword, die by the sword."

My mother's advice echoed in my mind, a mantra for survival. With a swift motion, I struck Tony in the nuts, sending Tony reeling, his shot firing harmlessly into the ceiling. I fled, jumping into the sanctuary of the empty swimming pool, pressing close to the wall. Silence enveloped me, a deafening void, until the world's sounds returned in sharp clarity.

The music's faint strains, the back door's creak, and the rustle of grass underfoot betrayed Tony's approach. "I will find you," he bellowed. My pulse thundered, a crescendo of fear, as the searing heat of a bullet tore through me. Time slowed, each detail etched with crystal precision—the leaves' dance in the breeze, the fiery pain in my chest, the struggle for breath. As I lay drowning on my own blood in an empty swimming pool, life's tapestry unraveled, leaving only the warmth of cherished memories to accompany the encroaching darkness.

The Beginning

The monotonous beep of the heart monitor cut through the silence, a stark counterpoint to the fog clouding my consciousness. The sterile tang of antiseptic hung heavy in the air, a harsh welcome as awareness crept in. My eyelids, leaden with the remnants of turmoil, fought against the intrusion of the stark hospital light. Blurred shapes slowly coalesced into clarity, and the drone of a news anchor filtered through, "The Big Fish apprehended at a New Jersey murder scene. An unidentified teen in critical condition in Brooklyn, now under protective custody." Panic clawed at my insides, but the ventilator's tube rendered me voiceless. Then, a touch of grace—my mother's voice, a whisper of love, and Evelyn's hand in mine.

I yearned to reassure them, to confess my regrets and reveal our newfound fortune. The hum of machinery melded with the crispness of the sheets against my skin. Fear swiftly gave way to a surge of anger as memories battered my senses—the unforgiving tiles of the swimming pool, the haunting reverberation of a gunshot, and the agony that had pierced my body. Fingers probing the bandages encircling my torso, I traced the trajectory of the bullet. The truth struck with brutal force—I had been shot. The details of that fateful night were as vivid as the fluorescent glare above, yet my mind grappled with the betrayal. A soft creak announced the arrival of a figure in scrubs—a nurse, or perhaps a doctor. Their visage, initially a blur, sharpened as they drew near.

A deluge of questions threatened to burst forth, but my parched throat betrayed me. "Easy there," they soothed. "Take it slow." I sank back into the pillows, the sedatives pulling me under once more. Why did he shoot me? I had complied with every demand. Why? The realization crept in—it had all been a setup from the start. But why? My gaze fell upon the calendar. June 17th, 2003. Three days lost. At eighteen, I was now wealthy and unshackled... I had survived, reconciled with my mother, and life was looking up.

A year had elapsed, and Kevin was living his dream—free from guilt, pain, and brimming with love. He had even founded Turner Real Estate. Life was idyllic until a chilling call shattered the peace. A voice from the past hissed, "Count your days, for this time, you won't escape." Click... And thus begins Kevin's tale: How to Survive Drowning in an Empty Swimming Pool (Tony Must Die!)

www.ingramcontent.com/pod-product-compliance
Lightning Source LLC
Chambersburg PA
CBHW051214120626
46547CB00013B/1352